TURN IT AROUND!
There's No Room Here For Drugs

DAVE WINFIELD
with Eric Swenson

TURN IT AROUND!
There's No Room Here For Drugs

DAVE WINFIELD
with Eric Swenson

A Wellington Press Project

PaperJacks LTD.

TORONTO   NEW YORK

AN ORIGINAL

PaperJacks

TURN IT AROUND!
There's No Room Here For Drugs

PaperJacks LTD

330 STEELCASE RD. E., MARKHAM, ONT. L3R 2M1
210 FIFTH AVE., NEW YORK, N.Y. 10010

First edition published May, 1987

Cover photo by Bill Hickey courtesy of Image Bank
Back cover photo by A. Earl Brown
Cover design by Paolo Pepe
Text design by Jill Dinneen

ISBN 0-7701-0733-8

ACKNOWLEDGMENTS

The idea for this book began in 1985 when David Winfield decided to focus more attention on drug-abuse education and prevention personally and through the Winfield Foundation. As he became more involved in drug programs, he recognized the need for a book that would arm people with knowledge and propose strategies for action. He asked Eric Swenson, a writer with whom he had worked before, to write the book with him. Their work was made easier by Frankie Coates, Chief of Demand Reduction, Drug Enforcement Administration; Karl Koon, Program Director and Coordinator of the Winfield Foundation's Turn It Around! campaign; and Albert S. Frohman, friend and advisor, who was an early inspiration for focusing on the drug problem. Merilyn Hatheway, although a loyal Red Sox fan, proved a devoted manuscript typist. Bobbie Elliott was an effective pinch hitter in the final inning of manuscript production. The enthusiasm and flexibility of the PaperJacks team—Susan Stoddart, president; Tony Seidl, publisher, Jim Connor, editor, and Chris Kingsley, coordinator—were remarkable. Rick Wolff and Brian L. P. Zevnik introduced the book to PaperJacks. The U.S. Department of Education and Texans' War on Drugs contributed to the chapter on Recommended Resources. The National Institute on Drug Abuse provided information on specific drugs and current research. The Drug Enforcement Administration supplied photographs, as did A. Earl Brown of Newark, NJ. Our thanks to all these agencies, organizations, and individuals.

—David M. Winfield,
Eric D. Swenson

Fort Lauderdale, Florida
April 3, 1987

NOTE: Although a collaborative effort, this book reflects the experiences of David Winfield and is written in the first-person singular.

CONTENTS

1. INTRODUCTION

The journey of a thousand miles begins with a single step.

—Chinese proverb

Setting Goals

My goal in writing this book is to produce a comprehensive yet succinct guide on how to fight substance abuse that can be understood, appreciated, and used by both young people and adults alike. I appreciate versatility as well as universality. I want the work to be a tool in the hands of many people trying to cope with drugs in America. This book will combine the elements I believe essential in dealing with the problem:

1. Incorporating the newest evidence discovered by research into addiction, drug-abuse prevention, and treatment
2. Considering new models that are proving effective—or at least promising—in preventing and combating drug abuse
3. Learning from the failures of past drug education and therapy programs, particularly in the historical context of drug use in America
4. Suggesting strategies to involve broad segments of the community in the effort to turn the drug problem around

The war on drugs has too frequently proven the maxim: "In war, truth is the first casualty." If the war on drugs is to be won, it will not be with propaganda and misinformation, but with facts and the truth. I believe this book contains the

1

essential information to making intelligent decisions about how best to fight drugs.

Alarming Trends

Knowledge I've gained from discussions at schools, visits to research facilities, prisons, government agencies, and rehabilitation centers is incorporated here. I've also read, reviewed, and analyzed the best available information. As I did so, I became alarmed by current trends. Today in America, drug potency, availability, use, and mortality are on the rise. On the flip side, prices, motivation, and morale are down. I bring a perspective of one who has seen the drug problem in the Far East, Latin America, and the Caribbean. I want this book to prove useful in such institutions as schools, city halls, service organizations, and churches in communities of all sizes. But, most importantly, I hope it will find a prominent place in the home and not just gather dust on a shelf. The role of the family in the fight against drugs cannot be overemphasized. This book is my best shot at sharing what I have learned and suggesting up-to-date strategies for the prevention and treatment of drug abuse and positive alternatives to the current problem.

Dave Winfield, Baseball Player

There are many questions I hope this book will answer. Perhaps the one I should start with is: Why am I, an outfielder for the New York Yankees, writing a book about drugs? As an athlete I have seen sports come under increased scrutiny and criticism for its use of drugs. I believe that drug abuse is only slightly more widespread among athletes than other segments of society. Even though athletes have high salaries, a lot of leisure time, and intense job pressures not found outside sports, there is now a wider knowledge and fear—at least in baseball—of what you lose if you use drugs. I have served as player representative for the Yankees and the San Diego

Padres and know the pulse of the industry of which I've been a member for almost fifteen years. I have seen the toll that drugs exact on professional athletes and have been in the front lines of clubhouse meetings and during the off season in trying to create drug policies that are fair to both players and owners *and* responsive to public concerns.

Because of our prominence, professional and even college athletes can play a significant role in turning the drug problem around. Whether or not we are capable or comfortable in the role, millions of Americans, especially youngsters, look up to us. Athletes have a platform from which to speak, a pedestal upon which we have been placed, that few others in America can command. I have used this platform in the past and will continue to use it. Being a role model is a responsibility and trust that I have never shirked. As an amateur and professional athlete, I've been a member of a team for twenty-five years and a leader on and off the field for almost as long. Helping to shape and influence young people and being a positive catalyst are only parts of the job for me. Today it has become even harder to trust individuals; we are all flawed humans with our own problems and agendas. But I am prepared to help take the lead on the drug question, to be a part of the team that helps restore faith in our institutions, and work to ensure that our institutions truly serve the public and deserve our faith.

Taking Care of Business

I am also a businessman, employing more than 300 people, and an employer who understands the importance of a healthy work force. But one doesn't have to be in business to appreciate that drug abuse results in an estimated $30 billion-a-year drain on our national wealth due to lost productivity. Unfortunately, such a statistic often remains impersonal, like the national debt and the trade deficit, and lost productivity is a heavy contributor to both. But, if our eyes are open, employers and employees of large and small firms alike can see the individual and collective casualties out there. They mount up.

Perennial All Star Winfield watches one fly.

Drug statistics are staggering. Thirty-five million Americans spend $110 billion annually to support illegal drug habits. One-quarter of our nation, including over half of our youth, has at least tried marijuana. Two out of three federal prisoners are in jail on drug-related violations. Despite spending billions of dollars trying to cut drugs off at our borders and keep them from our streets, it is a major accomplishment if even fifteen percent of the traffic in illegal drugs is stopped. Legal drugs are another part of the problem. More Americans abuse alcohol than any other drug. Sixty percent of our traffic fatalities are caused by drunk drivers. Last year 350,000 Americans died because of their addiction to nicotine. The cost to the public and private sectors, to families and individuals affected by drugs, is truly incalculable. Especially distressing to me is the loss of spirit and ambition among our youth that I see almost daily. Distracted and sidetracked by drugs, they are not becoming what they can be, which means that we as a nation are not reaching our potential. Many parents are caught up in this cycle and do not help out.

Being a Good Citizen

Finally, it is as a private citizen, as an individual wishing to do my part in a national team effort, that I wrote this book. No single person or organization can accomplish the task of turning people away from drugs. Changing values and behavior are slow and arduous undertakings, but they begin with a personal decision to act. What follows can be compared to a ripple effect as more people work in ever-widening circles. I hope my book will help refine and focus the many, often splintered efforts that characterize our attempt to deal with a massive national problem.

Solutions to the drug problem will vary according to time and place as the drug scene changes. Awareness of local conditions and local control is essential to effective drug education. What works in the inner city of Newark probably will not be relevant in the rural areas of Minnesota. Nevertheless, a highly visible, long-haul national campaign to turn

San Diego honors a favorite Padre.

around the drug problem can assist in getting the job done. We must start with strong leadership, a consistent strategy, and cooperation of the media and advertising agencies. Let's be inspired by the recent successes of the nationwide grassroots fight against drunk driving. New laws were passed and enforced, judges got tougher, but most importantly, attitudes changed. Drinking lost some of its allure; getting drunk or driving while drunk is no longer as widely tolerated. Let's remember that while many factors have contributed to this fight, a major one was two people who got MADD! (MADD, Mothers Against Drunk Driving, was founded in 1982 by Donna Frascella and Beverly Solonche after Mrs. Solonche's son was killed by a drunk driver.) Committed individuals are the building blocks of successful group efforts.

Starting with individuals and families, working through our schools and communities, and continuing on to regional efforts that finally have an impact on the entire nation, we can turn the drug problem around and in the process become far stronger as individuals and as a country. America faces a variety of pathologies, but substance abuse is the only illness I know in which the patient *and the family* are better after successful treatment than they were before the disease started. The Chinese present us with another way of looking at this phenomenon. Their word for crisis consists of two characters: One means danger, the other means opportunity. Let's use this opportunity to control our destiny and create a better future.

TURN IT AROUND
David M. Winfield Foundation

2. THE WINFIELD FOUNDATION/ TURN IT AROUND! CAMPAIGN

The starting point for a better world is the belief that it is possible. Civilization begins in the imagination. The wild dream is the first step to reality. Visions and ideas are potent only when they are shared. Until then, they are merely a form of daydreaming.

—Norman Cousins

Modest Beginnings

The Winfield Foundation is an organization that's now ten years old, with an office and professional staff in Fort Lee, New Jersey. We've carried out programs in several states with principal focus being the New York metropolitan area. But let me tell you how it started. When I left the University of Minnesota in 1973, I knew I was entering a new and challenging phase of life. I had been named a Williams Scholar in political science and, despite playing two major sports, had done well academically. Minnesota had given me a very good education. But now I was out there in the real world.

In college sports, things could hardly have gone better for me. It was like a dream come true. I had played key roles in Minnesota, winning the Big Ten Championship in both baseball and basketball. On the diamond, I was team captain and an All American as a pitcher. We were semi-finalists in the College World Series, for which I was named Most Valuable Player. For the first and only time in history, a young man was drafted by three different professional sports—football's Minnesota Vikings, the NBA's Atlanta Hawks and ABA's Utah Jazz, and baseball's San Diego Padres. I chose the Padres because I wanted to play baseball.

9

Kicking off the Turn It Around! campaign, Norfolk, Virginia, February 25, 1987.

My Commitment

I went straight from college to the major leagues without seasoning in the minors. At the beginning of my new career, I was filled with ambition and guarded self-confidence, but I realized that it was more than my own determination, discipline, and hard work that had gotten me where I was. I was uncertain how much could be chalked up to luck or politics, but one thing was for sure: Other people played a critical role in molding me—teachers, friends, family, coaches. They all contributed to my success and helped me become who I was in life. I wanted to continue that process by doing the same for others. People looked up to me and I asked myself: "What can I do to help someone else make it?" I thought of giving away baseballs, bats, basketballs, and other sports equipment at playgrounds, but then reconsidered and started what was more significant: a scholarship program in my hometown, St. Paul, Minnesota.

I gathered together some of my friends and we developed criteria for the award: excellence in academics, sports, and community service. I donated $1,000 from my first year's salary of $15,000 and we gave an awards dinner for our first two recipients, a girl and a boy. It was not a full-tuition scholarship, but rather an incentive and recognition for St. Paul's minority student athletes who had the ability and wanted to succeed. If they had worked and given to their community, then they would receive. It was this first effort that eventually led to the founding of the Winfield Foundation. We still maintain that program and now give out ten awards per year for those young "All Star" citizens.

San Diego and Beyond

In California I set up what became known in baseball as the Pavilion Program. In the first year, approximately 25,000 underprivileged and other kids came free to what is now Jack Murphy Stadium to watch baseball. As the idea grew, people started donating money and gifts. Volunteers gave their time and I realized then that we had to have better organization. I went through the Internal Revenue Service, filed legal applications, developed bylaws and guidelines, gained approval, and in 1977 the David M. Winfield Foundation was formed.

I made the priorities of the foundation the things that were important to me and had been my keys to success: health, education, and sports. We adopted the motto "A Sound Mind in a Sound Body." The Pavilion Program continued and expanded to not only my home stadium and various cities around the country, but also to the annual Major League Baseball All Star Game. The foundation has sponsored young people on athletic and cultural trips to cities such as Seattle, Minneapolis, San Diego, Houston, and Montreal. The scholarship program eventually included New York. Since 1982, we've awarded about $50,000 annually to New York City and St. Paul high school seniors. Together with the New York *Daily News,* the foundation provides scholarship awards for several all-city competitions—the spelling bee; art expo; orchestra, chorus, and band; science competition; and Golden Gloves. We've also sponsored computer literacy programs and a summer camp.

Our Children's Health

For several years the foundation has hosted health fairs throughout the New York region, as well as in the Minnesota Twin Cities and in San Diego, to bring physicians and other professionals into various communities or to the stadiums to provide services and promote better health habits. I've learned from and worked with medical centers such as the Columbia-Presbyterian Medical Center in New York, Bronx Lebanon Hospital, Scripps Clinic, the Mayo Clinic in Rochester, Minnesota, and the Minneapolis Health Department. In conjunction with the Hackensack Medical Center, which is the largest health-care delivery system in northern New Jersey, we offer nutritional screenings and counseling to both children and adults and actively promote health, fitness, and nutrition, through the media. Programs in weight control, stress management, and nutrition awareness are provided to communities, corporations, and individuals.

The more I work with kids and the more I travel, the more I come to realize that the greatest danger to their health and well-being, both physical and mental, is drugs. In 1985 I decided a drug-awareness program should become the principal focus of the foundation. Last year we sponsored more than forty school drug education programs in the New York metropolitan area. Building on the importance children bestow on athletes as role models, we brought sports figures like Willie Randolph, Bob Tewksbury, Dave Righetti, Jim Rice, Don Baylor, and Mark Breland into school assembly programs to help deliver the message. Many entertainers —among them Bill Cosby, Bobbi Humphrey, Kool and the Gang, Chuck Mangione, and Phoebe Snow—also contributed their time to these and other supporting events.

With the Drug Enforcement Administration, the foundation produced its first drug education video, which I narrated. It was beamed by satellite to more than 900 American television stations and carried on C-Span and cable networks. Translated into fourteen foreign languages, it has since been shown around the world. I am working with the DEA's newly created Demand Reduction Section and their Sports Drug Awareness Program to get coaches and athletes to "Team Up Against Drugs." They are an ever-growing nucleus of professionals with solid capabilities to address the task at hand. My speeches, public service messages, conferences, and seminars —all these activities occurred amid growing recognition in many quarters of just how serious the drug problem is.

Increasing Awareness

In 1986, a nationwide drive began to make the public, especially young people, aware of the dangers of drug abuse. The deaths of super athletes Len Bias and Don Rogers

Thumbs up on the Turn It Around! campaign

shocked not just sports fans, but the entire nation. The DEA now speaks of the "pre-Bias" and "post-Bias" periods of the war on drugs. President and Mrs. Ronald Reagan made joint and individual efforts to support the drive and create a greater national awareness of the problem. I applauded them for initiating such a critical endeavor. The United States Congress passed the most comprehensive anti-drug bill in its history. Broadcast and print journalists devoted unprecedented attention and time to the drug problem. Even Commissioner of Baseball Peter Ueberroth has a plan to block the importing of drugs into this country by cutting off foreign aid to supplier countries. As a result, the message of "JUST SAY NO" to drugs has reached nearly everyone, not only in this nation but in many other countries as well. Despite these efforts and a stepped-up battle to keep drugs out of this country, there are still more than 35,000,000 people in the U.S. using illegal drugs. If people continue to demand them, they can get them, they will sell them, they will use them. Clearly, something more must be done. Through the Winfield Foundation I have initiated one possible means of moving our nation toward the next step—the Turn It Around! campaign.

Turn it Around

The initial idea for a plan that would move beyond raising awareness occurred to me one evening in Connecticut. I had given a speech to more than 500 people at the Hi-Ho Mall in Bridgeport. Before my talk, several people had spoken to me about their individual and community inabilities—and frustrations—at not being able to deal with the drug menace.

The mayor introduced me, and the chief of police was also there. The citizens were concerned and attentive, looking for a message, an answer for their town. They were also lively, like at a ball game, and had given the two public officials a round of boos. Near the end of what I would call a rousing speech, I asked these two gentlemen to join me. I put my arms around them and told the crowd that regardless of what they thought

New York's Mayor Koch with Dave Winfield Foundation Scholarship winners.

of the politics and methods of the mayor and the police chief, we all had one thing in common: We were all together in the fight against drugs and we had to be united if we were going to turn it around. The crowd roared in approval.

It was a good speech and I was still exhilarated during the car ride home. A foundation staffer and I analyzed the talk and kept coming back to the themes of unity, the need to reverse the trend of drug abuse, and the phrase "turn it around." In my mind's eye, I saw a thermometer with the temperature climbing higher and higher, representing the nation's drug use. Perhaps it was beginning to level off, but that wasn't good enough. That temperature was much too high. Drug abuse had to be turned around. We needed more than words; we needed to translate awareness into action. We began to plan a second stage for our efforts.

The goals we established for the new campaign were to:

1. Focus community attention on the problem of substance abuse.

2. Harness the resources of the community in order to create a spirit of cooperation.

3. Bring together community leaders and local resources in order to combat drug abuse in a positive and non-threatening way.

4. Establish a partnership linking adult leaders in the community with students and local youth groups.

5. Educate the community on substance abuse by using materials designed specifically for the parent, teacher, and student.

6. Create a framework for future leaders of the community by involving students in the process from the outset.

7. Give youngsters viable alternatives to drug use by building individual self-esteem and by providing positive role models.

8. Create a mutual information and referral system for students and the community as a whole.

9. Develop a reward and recognition system —for example, a yearly event—in order to promote community involvement and to enhance self-esteem.
10. Develop a method of gathering data from the community before and during the campaign to monitor drug usage.

The Next Step

In establishing a comprehensive community effort to eradicate drug abuse, it becomes necessary to move from an individual awareness of drug abuse to community-wide awareness, and then provide action as encompassed in the Turn It Around! Campaign. This national effort will provide a variety of positive alternatives to young people as a way of enhancing their self-esteem, as well as providing exciting opportunities for personal growth and development. Armed with knowledge, trained for leadership, and inspired to do service, our youth can achieve their potential and be part of the team that contributes significantly to solving real problems.

The Turn It Around! Campaign consists of three major components. The primary component of the entire campaign is the Community Partnership. This partnership is designed to combine the efforts and expertise of a cross-section of the community—people committed to taking a stand against drug abuse and the problems that cause drug abuse in their area. The partnership serves as both a resource bank and a core group for each community's campaign. Each partnership will have representatives from the local clergy, city government, medical community, school system (students and faculty), parents, law and justice systems, businesses, celebrities, the media, and local non-profit organizations. Each group represented by the partnership's core committee will have specific responsibilities and commitments to ensure the campaign's success in the respective community.

As the organizing unit in a community, some of the responsibilities of the partnership core group include:

- Identify and confirm local leadership.
- Plan a specific yearly curriculum for the local campaign.
- Develop a contract/covenant and timetable for implementation for each group represented on the partnership.
- Develop a reward and recognition system for the campaign in the community.
- Maintain statistics and records on the process —specifically, preprogram baseline information, updates, and future plans.
- Focus attention and action on issues impacting the community.

The major thrust of the partnership in a community will be the active involvement and participation of students from the local schools in community service projects, volunteer positions, or student employment in local businesses. In addition, students will complete monthly projects as determined by national campaign guidelines.

Networking the Nation

The second component of the Turn It Around! Campaign is sponsoring an annual national youth conference, the first of which is scheduled for autumn, 1987. At this conference, high school students from across the nation will meet in Washington, D.C., to identify, analyze, and recommend solutions to mutually shared problems they encounter in their respective communities. During the week, participants will attend workshops on problem-solving techniques; leadership development; drug education and awareness; handling stress and coping with change. Plans for the first conference also include submitting a position paper to Congress and the President on the findings and recommendations of the participants. Future conferences will be attended by students who have won competitions sponsored by Turn It Around! Community partnerships across the country, as well as exemplary repre-

Dave's buddies in the pavilion, Yankee Stadium.

sentatives from other programs. This opportunity for participants to network with their peers from across the nation will also establish connections for future partnerships in cities across the country.

Creating New Tools

The final component of the Turn It Around! Campaign is the development of up-to-date educational videos and materials that will provide guidance in implementing and maintaining the partnerships in a community. I view this book as one of these tools. It is essential that the fast, ever-changing information pertaining to the drug scene not only be current, but be developed to include children who are young enough to be positively influenced before they participate in drug use. The average age of young people who first experiment with drugs is twelve and a half. Realizing that drug abuse is taking its toll at an even earlier age, the Winfield Foundation is committed to getting information to younger people in an effort to curb this pervasive problem. The next video we produce will be used to help educate students in kindergarten through sixth grade in a way that is enlightening as well as entertaining. We will also produce a video appropriate for older students and adults. Both will be complemented by written materials for parents and teachers.

The Winfield Foundation realizes that this campaign is a massive undertaking that cannot be entered into lightly or for the short term if it is to succeed. The foundation's role in the Turn It Around! Campaign will be to develop the program and to offer a tested, comprehensive, and successful model program to communities and schools across the nation. In addition, the foundation will serve as a recruiting organization to locate local organizations to initiate the program in their communities, and will serve as the national liaison for all community partnerships. The foundation also will act as consultants to assist requesting schools, cities, regions, and the like.

A Positive Approach

In essence, the Turn It Around! Campaign is designed to establish or reestablish positive values at all community levels and inspire leadership from within and from the grassroots. Only through participation and reinforcement are new values developed and accepted. Therefore, the next step after drug awareness requires that our youth become actively involved in programs that demonstrate positive alternatives and alter life-styles and their underlying philosophies. Our nation's young people need hands-on experience in determining their future role in society, while under the nurturing guidance of competent adults. Drugs are a negative force that subtract from the user's abilities and divide the user and the community. Our campaign allows participants to add to the anti-drug effort and multiply its effect.

The Turn It Around! Campaign proposes to form community partnerships that will actively seek to provide the youth of the nation with positive examples and experiences. Much like Robert Baden-Powell and Juliette Low, founders of the Boy Scouts and Girl Scouts, respectively, the Winfield Foundation envisions a campaign geared toward allowing young people to practice positive values in a cooperative environment.

Communities wishing to learn more about the Turn It Around! Campaign should write:

> The David M. Winfield Foundation
> 2050 Center Avenue
> Fort Lee, NY 07024

3. STRATEGIES FOR ACTION

A War on Many Fronts

Although I have never served in the armed forces, as a veteran campaigner in the war on drugs I am beginning to better appreciate the intricacies of military strategy. Certainly we are engaged in a large-scale combat operation fought on several fronts that requires close overall planning. I would identify those fronts as: research, education, treatment, and enforcement. Should we fail on any one of these fronts, we risk losing on the others, for all of them are linked.

Treatment, for instance, is just as important to drug-abuse prevention as is education. Every untreated user is literally or figuratively a salesperson for drugs and, at the same time, a

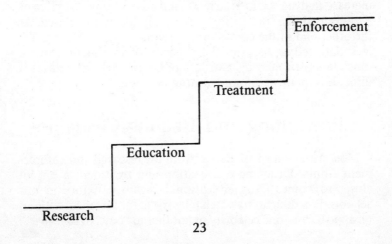

buyer, always escalating the crime. We could construct a hierarchy of steps that might clarify the relationship between the four components of drug-abuse prevention.

At the bottom, research underlies the other components, providing new methods of approaching the other steps and monitoring their effectiveness. The more steps we must take to counter drugs, the more expensive the job becomes and the harder it is to achieve results. The wisdom of such folk sayings as "a stitch in time saves nine" or "an ounce of prevention is worth a pound of cure" should be apparent, but is seldom applied when we budget resources.

To return to the metaphor of war, the front under greatest pressure is enforcement. Here we fight a constant rearguard action and it is easy to see why drug exports continue to be a major source of unofficial income for poor, Third World countries. With 30,000 miles of border and coastline, U.S. authorities are stretched thin and hard pressed to cut off the flow of drugs before they reach us. Even after drug traffickers are caught, they often are punished lightly or slip through an overburdened criminal justice system. In ten years there has been a forty percent increase in our prison population nationally. New York State went from 17,000 to 35,000 inmates; Florida from 19,000 to 32,000. Seventy-five percent of all court cases in southern Florida are drug-related. Despite the increase in drug seizures, arrests, and convictions, the price of cocaine is down, indicating that supply has not declined. At the other end of the continuum, research is also suffering. We lack data telling us even the capacity of treatment centers, much less their efficacy. Our lack of benchmark data makes it difficult to plan well-founded drug policies.

Preventing and Treating Casualties

Most Americans feel distant from the research and enforcement fronts. Drug-abuse education and treatment are a lot closer to home. Drug education is again a fixture in our schools. It is difficult to watch television, for instance, without an appeal from one celebrity or another to "Say No to Drugs."

It is estimated that every drug addict has a direct effect on four other individuals. There are few among us who haven't been touched in some way.

If there is anywhere the image of war is inappropriate, it is when we talk of addicts. They are front-line casualties, and it is counterproductive to treat them with hatred. Jerome Jaffee, director of the National Addiction Research Center, points out the dilemma: "If we say drug use is something we don't tolerate, on the one hand we deter it, but on the other hand we stigmatize users," reducing their chance of recovery. Also threatening the chances of recovery are the limited number of "slots" in public-sector treatment centers. Almost all have long waiting lists. While there are empty beds in private hospitals, many addicts lack sufficient medical insurance and cannot afford daily room rates of $200 to $800. America's ambivalence to addicts is shown by a recent Gallup poll. Forty-two percent of the respondents said the government should make educating young people about drug dangers its top priority. Only four percent felt the top priority should be helping addicts overcome their disease. It is difficult not to be ambivalent toward addicts in view of their many crimes and other antisocial acts. My native state of Minnesota has long been a leader in providing responsive and compassionate public care for addicts. Peter Bell and Peter Hayden were pioneers in providing care to indigent and black abusers. The private sector has also achieved attention with the Hazeltine treatment facility, for example, contracting with the National Football League to care for drug abusing players.

Getting Involved

Members of the general public may feel that research and enforcement are beyond them and best left to others or to the government. I disagree. I'm reminded of the late President Eisenhower's observation that the people's desire for peace was so strong that the government had better step aside and let them have it. How strong is our desire to turn around the drug problem in America? Is it strong enough to inspire us to

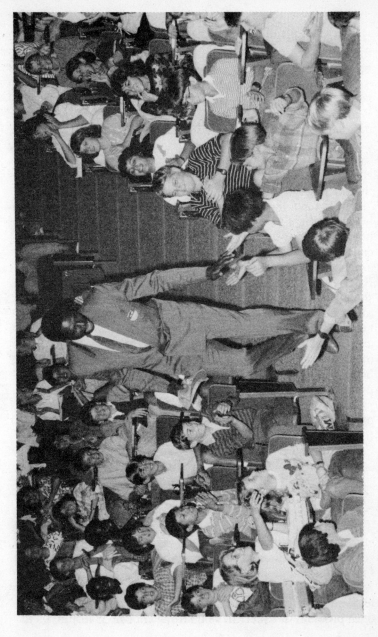

Kids—Dave's favorite audience. Appearance in Fairfax, Virginia, with DEA Chief John Lawn.

responsibilities we've never before assumed? Take the question of research. How can you know the kind or extent of drug use in your community or school system if that use is not measured? How can you determine whether you are turning the problem around unless you continue to monitor? The anonymous survey is a basic tool in this effort. An excellent model is the annual survey of drug use among high school seniors conducted by the University of Michigan Institute for Social Research. Law enforcement officials can also be involved in determining drug-abuse patterns through arrest records and other means.

Enforcement is an area that even schoolchildren can become a part of. Who can better check drug use on school grounds or adjacent areas? Students, faculty, administration, and the police working together can. Neighborhood watch programs have proved effective in deterring burglaries. Let's use them to deter drug sales and usage. Knowing what to look for and having a commitment to being involved are the keys. The courts also bear watching. Monitor and document how drug-related cases are handled in your community. What messages do your courts send to criminals and the community? Make sure judges and juries recognize your concern. A court-watch program is a good way to involve retired members of your community. Citizens can also go beyond encouraging effective enforcement to lobbying for better laws. Laws banning drug paraphernalia sales are one example of local efforts to discourage drug use.

Educating the community about drugs can take place at many levels for different audiences. Most schools already have specific drug abuse education programs, but teachers can instruct students about the subject in several regular academic courses—the effects of drugs on the body and brain in biology and chemistry; the international dimensions of the problem in social studies; past trends of drug use in history classes. Certainly driver education courses should stress the impairment caused by drugs. High school students teaching junior high students, who then instruct elementary pupils, is an effective way of capitalizing on the regard of younger children for older ones. We're all role models to someone.

Outside the school, drug and alcohol information programs can be set up. Parents can assist other parents in family life skills courses, seminars, workshops, and conferences. These forums are excellent recruiting and training sites. Regular or special programming on local cable television stations can be scheduled.

Some kinds of treatment can also be assisted by non-professionals. Support groups for children of alcoholics, who are at high risk as substance abusers, are an example. We can also help to reintegrate reforming users into the school, community or workplace.

Mobilizing the Community

If your community does not have an organization or project devoted to sponsoring abuse prevention programs, start one. This usually begins with one person—or a few—reaching out to others. If there is a drug problem in your town, turn it around; if there isn't, keep it down. Don't let fear of failure deter you—and in one way, I can speak as an expert on failing. More than seven out of every ten times when I come to the plate, I make an out. You should not be discouraged if your efforts lead to no apparent success.

Using conventional research methods, it is difficult to evaluate precisely the effect of multifaceted community programs to counter substance abuse. With so many factors to be considered and the difficulty of achieving a control group, such programs must be measured using less formal evidence. Few people would deny, however, that a highly visible program such as Mothers Against Drunk Driving (MADD) and the student group (SADD) are making a difference. Such organizations have succeeded in raising the level of concern and awareness and in reducing tolerance for substance abuse in the media and among peers and the community.

Although these efforts frequently begin with parents of school-aged children, they must enlist other community members in order to gain the wide support that is the foundation for changing attitudes. Professional organizations including those in medicine, pharmacology, and education have, and are establishing, programs to increase the ability of the membership to assist in the war on drugs. Because no member of the community is unaffected by drugs, every member is a potential partner.

In pulling together the group that will support your efforts, include youth from the start. They are your primary audience, and the cross-generational dynamic is an exciting one. Some community members are in a strategic position to contribute. I'd like to make a special appeal to doctors, particularly family practioners, to join or start coalitions to fight drugs. They are often leaders in their community, serve as physicians to sporting teams, and know both children and their parents. They are also in a position to detect current and potential drug users.

Look for ways to network with other community groups immediately. Literally thousands of substance abuse programs have developed in the last decade. Much or all of what you might need—advice, material, trainers—is available, and perhaps even close by. Joint projects are one way of having a greater effect at less cost.

As projects get started, don't concentrate on the product or client and neglect the process. Does your group work in a supportive and caring environment? While you may assume that everyone in your group shares a common concern, can you help them to have a deeper motivation? Consider projects that are not directly drug-related. If service is a value you wish to promote, there are many ways to serve.

The Special Role of Parents

There's no doubt that parenting has become a lot more difficult for Americans, even compared to when I was growing up. To begin with, many are doing the job alone. The typical family of generations past—working father, with mother at home—has very nearly disappeared from the scene. Only one family in twenty follows this traditional path. Almost two families out of five are headed by single parents, making their

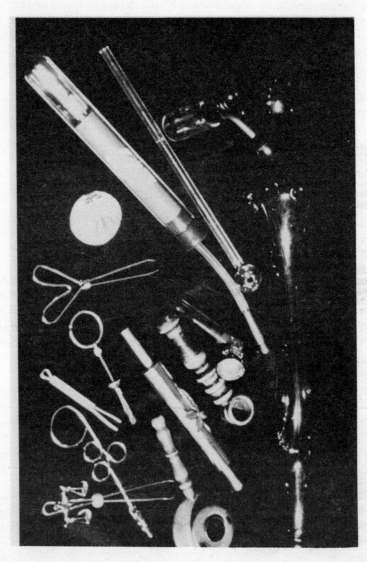

Marijuana paraphernalia.   Are these items on sale in your community?

task doubly hard. In some families television has become a surrogate parent with greater influence than natural parents. These changes in child-rearing have contributed not only to drug use, but to other problems as well. The job of preventing drug use begins at home. I suggest parents examine the role they play in encouraging or discouraging it. We hear a lot about athletes as role models, particularly when they fail, but the effect we can have on your children is minuscule compared to the effect you can have on them. Ask yourself some questions:

Do you talk one way and walk another? Are you honest or hypocritical? What is the example of drug use that you set in the home?

Do you set clear and consistent rules for behavior and then enforce them? Do you lack direction and confuse the child by being too lax or too severe, or both on different occasions? Do you know that excessive criticism or lack of approval are associated with drug abuse in children?

Do you give your children daily responsibilities to encourage self-discipline? In what ways do you hold them accountable for their acts? Do you establish standards for their unsupervised activities?

How well do you know your children's friends, their activities, and their whereabouts? Do you communicate regularly with the parents of your children's friends? Do you chaperone social events for your children and encourage other parents to do the same?

How well do you communicate with your children? Are you available? Nonjudgmental? Objective? Do you accept your child and refrain from nagging and attacking?

Parents are in the front line of the war against drug abuse. How they fare will largely determine the fate for all of us. My advice to them and the community at large is based on common sense, discipline and caring. There are no magic formulas here—just hard work with vast rewards. My hope is that this book will help people to have a better intellectual grasp of the problem and move them to act. With the right leadership and an emerging consensus, we can save ourselves years of pain and fear caused by drug abuse and turn the problem around.

4. A SHORT HISTORY OF DRUG USE IN AMERICA

Those who do not learn from history are condemned to repeat it.

—George Santayana

I have done a great deal of research in the course of educating myself about drugs. It was, at times, almost like going back to school. In fact, for a short while I did go back to school at Quantico, Virginia. This is where potential DEA and FBI agents learn their trade and about drugs as well. Visits to the University of California Medical School at Irvine, the Mayo Clinic, and the Hackensack Medical Center were part of the process. As I prepared to play a more active role in drug-awareness programs, a major motivator for me was the desire to go before the public with a comprehensive knowledge of the problem. I've faced audiences of several thousand and appeared on live television before tens of thousands, and I sure didn't want to be unprepared or appear foolish. I didn't want the audience to know more about drugs than I did (and you probably would be surprised at how much even young kids know about drugs).

One of the subjects that fascinated me was how we got to where we are today regarding drugs. If the past is prologue to the present, what could we learn from history? How can we know where we're going unless we know where we've been? I was surprised to learn, for instance, that we are now in the second national cocaine epidemic, the first having occurred between 1885 and 1905. New laws and a vigorous public education campaign helped end cocaine's hold the first time. Understanding the cyclical nature of drug patterns may also help us to better control them. We can also learn from what

Special Agent Winfield. Graduation day at the FBI Academy in Quantico.

one researcher has aptly called "the drug problem problem" —the damage resulting from how society has dealt with the drug problem.

The Early Americans

Even before the arrival of Europeans in the Americas, there was widespread drug usage here. In fact, pre-Columbian American Indians had the broadest range of drugs in the world. Hallucinatory, ecstatic-trance states were essential parts of the Indian religious experience and were often achieved through use of psychedelic drugs. (Several of these —such as peyote, mescaline, morning glory seeds, and psilocybin—were popular in the 1960s.) Ironically, with all this availability, it was not until the Colonists introduced alcohol to the Indians that the native population encountered a drug problem, one that still remains today.

Tobacco was the most commonly used drug in the New World. After Columbus returned to Europe with a supply of leaves and seeds, tobacco spread rapidly to the other continents. Smoking is a uniquely American contribution to the global drug culture. It is difficult to imagine how the early economic development of America would have proceeded without a heavy reliance on drugs. In New England the infamous "Triangular Trade" developed. There, rum was distilled and shipped to Africa to be traded for slaves who were taken to the West Indies and bartered for molasses, which was returned to New England to start the cycle anew. Many slaves, of course, came to the American South, where their initial primary task became the cultivation of tobacco. By the mid-eighteenth century tobacco was the principal export of the North American colonies.

Marijuana was another early American cash crop, although it was originally grown as rope fiber. Both presidents Washington and Jefferson planted marijuana, and some scholars believe Washington actually used it as a drug. Well into the twentieth century marijuana was cultivated. It grew wild in practically every part of the land. It was not until the Roaring Twenties that the weed became disreputable. The history of drug regulation in this country is marked by the promotion of drugs that the establishment found socially acceptable and the prohibition of those drugs used by minorities. Mexican laborers in the Southwest and black musicians in New Orleans smoked marijuana, and in the mind of whites (even though they, too, smoked marijuana), it became associated with the low life, the deviant, and the criminal.

The Juice of the Poppy

Opium suffered a similar fate in the U.S. Brought to the colonies by the Pilgrims, the drug was widely prescribed for several ailments. Benjamin Rush, a physician and signer of the Declaration of Independence, recommended it for treating alcoholism. He reasoned that a patient was better off becoming addicted to a less dangerous drug. This use of opium continued until the 1940s in some parts of the U.S. Nineteenth-century American merchants derived immense profits by exporting opium into China. While it was the British who enjoyed the lion's share of this traffic, and who fought the opium wars in 1839–42 to preserve it, American interests were considerable. The Delanos, as in Franklin *Delano* Roosevelt, made a fortune in the opium trade. It was not until opium-smoking Chinese workers were brought to this country in the mid-nineteenth century that "problems" with the drug were reported.

Opium, through its derivative, morphine, first caused doctors to recognize addiction as a medical problem. Morphine addiction became so common among veterans of the Civil War that it became known as the "soldiers' disease." Widely used as a painkiller in the bloodiest war ever fought up to that time, opium begat a generation of men who needed their daily fix. By the early twentieth century opium use had greatly expanded. There were a million addicts in the U.S.—more than half of them women—who consumed more than 100,000 pounds of the drug annually. The usual sources were opiate-laden patent medicines. Other than their use in Chinese opium dens, which led to "Oriental depravity," opiates were not seen as a particular menace to society. According to a 1919 survey, seventy-five percent of our country's opium addicts were gainfully employed.

After the passage of the Harrison Anti-Narcotic Act in 1914 a full-scale anti-drug war was launched and the number of addicts steadily declined. Those who could not withdraw from opium turned to smugglers, and criminal trade in heroin from the Near East ensued. A new breed of criminals was created and pursued with a vigor not seen in any other nation. One result was that no nation faced anything even remotely as serious as the heroin problem that developed in the United States.

The Magical Drug

No single drug contributed to the passage of the Harrison Act as much as cocaine. Only three decades earlier, Sigmund Freud's extravagant praise of the drug in "On Coca" (he called it "magical" and recommended it to friends and patients) had helped popularize the substance. Cocaine supposedly improved the powers of the mind. Even Sir Arthur Conan Doyle turned his fictional detective Sherlock Holmes into a user. Cocaine use grew quickly as physicians freely prescribed it, often as a cure for other addictions. Patent-medicine manufacturers came to rely on it, and literally hundreds of medicines had a cocaine base. A popular drink of the day was Vin Mariani, composed of wine and coca. Personages such as Thomas Alva Edison, President William McKinley, and Pope Leo XIII became frequent users and endorsers of the product. In 1886, Coca-Cola was introduced to compete with Vin Mariani. It soon achieved worldwide popularity, and scores of other "soft" drinks based on coca appeared.

As with many other widely prescribed "wonder drugs," its initial popularity was replaced with a growing recognition that cocaine was a serious and often deadly health hazard. American medicine was increasingly concerned with raising professional standards and curbing patent-medicine use. More and more doctors began to speak out against the drug. It

Opium poppy—the world's oldest continuously used drug.

should be noted that public opinion against the drug was not rallied, however, until mass media and legislators joined the battle. They succeeded largely by tying cocaine use to crime, particularly among black people.

The first people to be called "dope fiends" were cocaine-using blacks. Articles in medical journals and the popular press, as well as speeches on the floor of Congress and state legislatures, hyped the threat. *The New York Times* charged that "Most attacks upon white women in the South . . . are the direct result of the coke-crazed Negro brain." Blacks using the drug were thought to be unaffected by a mere .32-caliber bullet, so Southern police departments switched to .38-caliber pistols! Dr. Hamilton Wright, the U.S. Representative to the 1910 Shanghai Conference on Narcotic Control, claimed that black misuse of cocaine was the greatest threat in the country.

Amid this hysteria, cocaine became the most feared drug in the U.S. State and federal laws banning cocaine were quickly passed and their penalties were more stringent than for other drugs. Limited use of the drug continued but was restricted almost exclusively to the ghetto and the "artistic" set. Cocaine went underground until the 1970s, when it reemerged, still illegal but with the mistaken reputation of being a "soft" drug for those who could afford it.

The Great Experiment

While the next drug to be prohibited was alcohol, the ban was relatively short-lived (1920–1933). Congress passed a constitutional amendment prohibiting the "manufacture, sale, transportation, importation, or exportation of intoxicating liquors" in 1917, in part as a temporary measure to save grain during World War I. By January 1919, the necessary thirty-two states had ratified the amendment, and one year later the law went into effect. The long fight against "ardent spirits" waged by the Women's Christian Temperance Union, the Prohibition Party, and others was won, but not for long.

The nation rebelled against Prohibition not because alcohol wasn't a dangerous drug, or because the laws weren't working

California's number one crop—sensimilla marijuana

to lower consumption and alcohol-related problems. What soon became apparent was that the cure was worse than the disease. Prohibition contributed to the rise of organized-crime syndicates, reckless and corrupt law enforcement, speakeasies, poisonous alcohol, greater use of other drugs, and widespread contempt for law and authority. Anyone seeking a blueprint for public-policy disaster should study this chapter of American history closely. Prohibition accomplished its intended goal, but with the cost of unintended development of new social problems such as organized crime, which continues to plague us. Trying to legislate morality or change strongly held patterns of social behavior by law, particularly without society's full cooperation, can backfire.

The Spreading Weed

One of the drugs that gained in popularity in the U.S. during this period was the previously seldom-used marijuana. Even so, relatively few people had heard of the drug when the Treasury Department created the Federal Narcotics Bureau in 1930. This situation was quickly remedied by Harry J. Anslinger, the bureau's first director who held the post until 1962.

Anslinger methodically set about to inform the public of marijuana's supposed dangers. In public lectures, radio addresses, magazine and newspaper articles, he hammered away at the foe in lurid terms, describing innumerable cases of murder, rape, and insanity that he ascribed to the drug. His work attracted reformers and moralists, particularly after the repeal of Prohibition. The mass media cooperated enthusiastically. Sensationalized accounts of the drug's dangers (with little effort to separate fact from fancy) appeared throughout the country. By 1937, less than seven years after the creation of the bureau, the nation was convinced that an epidemic existed and that a crime wave was imminent due to the use of the drug. Forty-six states had already enacted anti-marijuana legislation, and that year a federal marijuana bill was passed by Congress. The only medical testimony offered during the hearings on the bill was from a physician representing the AMA who opposed the act.

For the next quarter-century penalties for marijuana use were continually escalated and the media campaign intensified. Such camp classics as the film *Reefer Madness* were seriously promoted as hard-hitting drug-education programs. As the 1960s began, there were fewer than 200 federal arrests per year for marijuana possession or sales. Then came the dawning of the Age of Aquarius.

A Time of Change

During the 1960s and 1970s a revolution in American values, morals, culture, and institutions occurred. The Vietnam War, the assassinations of the Kennedys and Martin Luther King, Jr., the threat of nuclear war, and Watergate utterly changed our sense of nation and self. Music, television, and movies—entertainers and rock stars—played an accelerated role in changing our lives. Actors in popular films like *Easy Rider, Super Fly, Annie Hall,* and *Animal House* used drugs freely. *Up in Smoke* was entirely devoted to glorifying marijuana. Song lyrics often extolled drug use. The gap between generations, between the establishment and the counter-culture, was never wider, and no issue so characterized the split as drug use among the flower children. "Never trust anybody over thirty" became the motto of a new generation that seemed intent on and content with "turning on, tuning in, and dropping out."

No age had as full a drug cabinet. For the first time in history, *pro*-drug activists such as Dr. Timothy Leary, Ken Kesey, and Allen Ginsberg appeared on the scene. While the names may be unfamiliar to today's school-aged population, entertainment stars such as Jimi Hendrix, Janis Joplin, and Jim Morrison died of drug overdoses. Acid, speed, and pot use skyrocketed, as did heroin use, particularly after veterans returned from Vietnam, where tens of thousands of soldiers had become addicted to smack. Studies indicate the addiction rate was as high as twenty percent. Many soldiers turned to drugs to overcome the horror or boredom of the war in Vietnam. Some stayed on drugs after returning to the States, where their plight was for too long unrecognized. They returned to woefully inadequate rehabilitation and support programs. During this time drugs became big business. Today, for instance, marijuana is a major agricultural product in several states. According to the National Organization for the Reform of Marijuana Laws, it is a $16.6 billion-a-year industry, the second biggest crop in the country. None of this is taxed, of course, because it is in the black market, or underground economy. All this has occurred despite dramatically accelerated anti-drug legislation, education, and enforcement.

I'm actually heartened by what is happening in entertainment in the '80s. The industry appears to be cleaning up its act. Jerry Garcia, Eric Clapton and Jackson Browne are no longer singing "high on cocaine." There's actually a California group called Rock Against Drugs (what a RAD acronym). Drugs are still taking their toll on stars, however. David Crosby and Stacey Keach are recently out of prison on drug charges; Steve Howe, Lamar Hoyt, and Vida Blue are suspended from baseball; John Belushi is suspended from life.

Looking in the Mirror

The 1960s flower children are now on the other side of the generation gap and *their* children are facing an even tougher fight against drugs. If we are to succeed in helping them say no to drugs, we must learn from the mistakes of the past. Instead of looking for creative and effective solutions of treating what is at heart a medical problem within our communities, we have focused on trying to eliminate the supply and punishing the offender. That alone is a futile approach. Too often we have not understood the nature of addiction—the new metabolisms created by drug dependency, for instance. Sometimes our anti-drug campaigns have succeeded in replacing less harmful substances with more harmful substances. The misconceptions, distortions, and misinformation perpetrated by zealous reformers and the media have been worse than

Nineteenth century patent medicines for children and adults featured cocaine, opium, and heroin.

ineffective; they have been counterproductive. Let us learn that if drug education is to succeed, we must rationally and honestly look at our chemical society and at the role each of us plays in that society. We must learn the facts about drugs and we must tell the truth about drugs. In view of our nation's past experience with drugs, we should also consider that history is not destiny.

5. UNDERSTANDING ADDICTION

Addict: from Latin addictus, *"given over," one awarded to another as a slave.*

Rethinking the Problem

Why do people become addicts? This is another question that sent me to the books and to researchers. The answers I found certainly changed my understanding of the problem. There are many reasons why people take drugs. But why can some take them and then stop, while others find themselves unable to quit? The prevalent view is that all that is needed to solve the problem is for the addict to straighten out and fly right. This view, I learned, simply doesn't mesh with the facts. In the last few years scientists have made quantum leaps in their knowledge of how drugs affect the brain and how genes are the basis for many diseases. If you felt a bit like you were in the classroom during the previous chapter's history lesson, please keep your seats. In this period you will learn some biochemistry.

Forms of Addiction

Many types of addiction permeate our society. One powerful mind-altering device found in almost every American home is the television set. It is a sad fact that by the time the typical American child has graduated from high school he or she has spent more time in front of a television set than in a classroom. It would be harder for many Americans to get through a day without television than for a heroin addict to get through a day without a fix. The automobile is another

46

machine deemed absolutely essential to the life-style of the average American. Gambling, sex, work, and exercise are common activities that people often become addicted to. Food inspires a tremendous variety of obsessive behavior. The common features of all addictions are compulsion, repeated action, and the loss of control.

A New Science

Recent research into drug dependence has yielded much new evidence regarding how drugs take control of the addict's mind. Evidence is so dramatic and compelling that it has begun to utterly change the way responsible professionals deal with drug addicts. The new science of addictionology has emerged in this decade and is forcing the scientific community and thoughtful members of the general public to alter their attitudes toward addicts.

For years addicts have been considered as morally flawed irresponsible losers, whose antisocial compulsions and lack of self-control have caused incalculable harm to themselves, their loved ones, and society. As our research becomes more sophisticated and our comprehension grows, a new portrait of the addict emerges. It appears that addiction can be an inevitable result of an individual's body chemistry and one's exposure to drugs. The chemical dependencies created in the brain may be so powerful that the urge for the drug is stronger than even the will to survive. That is incredible but true!

Laboratory experiments with monkeys and rats show that the animals, if allowed to self-administer cocaine, will do so until they kill themselves. They will push a lever tens of thousands of times to get one hit of the drug. The animals will pass up food and water, and male rhesus monkeys will even ignore females in heat to get cocaine. Larger animals also find cocaine addictive and deadly. In 1986 a 300-pound bear in Tennessee who discovered a cocaine trafficker's stash and remained at the site eating his way through the drug until it killed him. These examples prove that addiction is not a condition unique to humans.

The Brain's Reward System

New research shows that the brain contains specialized reward mechanisms capable of controlling behavior. These mechanisms can be switched on by drugs. It may well be that even non-drug pleasures, such as those derived from food or sex, can become drug-controlled. This positive reward system appears to be far more important in motivating behavior than the negative-reinforcement mechanisms of physical dependence/withdrawal. The new evidence is a further development of earlier discoveries that the brain produces its own natural opiates called endorphins. Researchers at Johns Hopkins, led by Solomon Snyder, made this breakthrough discovery in 1973. Building on this work in the late 1970s, Mark Gold, M.D., a research psychiatrist, pioneered a safe, chemical, non-addictive treatment for opiate withdrawal. By finding the biochemical basis of withdrawal and treatment, Gold helped to force others to rethink centuries of theories regarding the diagnosis and care of addicts. Additional research by others yielded similar results.

The Genetic Link

Harvard psychiatrist George Vaillant's *Natural History of Alcoholism*, published in 1983, caused a stir in the medical and psychiatric communities. Begun in 1940 and tracing the lives of 600 adolescents before any drinking problems were present, his study showed that "Addiction, like a disease, has a life of its own and is not a moral or a psychological problem." Vaillant found that "alcoholics are depressed because they drink; they don't drink because they are depressed." One "enormous difference" between alcoholics and non-alcoholics was that "Many of the men [in the study] who developed alcoholism had alcoholic parents."

Researchers probed whether children became alcoholics through learned behavior or genetics. Investigations at medical schools in Kansas and Missouri focused on alcohol abuse by biological children of alcoholics who had been adopted as infants by other families. These children were three times as likely to develop the disease as the children of non-alcoholics. Other evidence also points to genetic forces, rather than psychological factors, in the development of dependence. The metabolism and enzyme production of severe alcoholics is different from that of moderate drinkers. Children of alcoholics often produce abnormal brain waves not found in non-alcoholics and their children. The huge majority of cocaine addicts come from alcoholic families, which suggests that addiction might be a genetic disease with the particular drug of choice up to the individual.

Mark Gold's research into cocaine continues to contradict the view of the addict as a moral degenerate with low self-esteem, major emotional problems, and a history of drug abuse. Callers to the National Cocaine Helpline, which Gold helped establish in my home state of New Jersey, revealed a different profile entirely. In three years the Helpline received more than 1,500,000 calls. The average user was a twenty-five-year-old college-educated white professional earning more than $25,000 a year, with no prior history of emotional problems or drug abuse.

Drugs and Their Effects

Knowing the facts is the first step toward solving a problem, and the following section covers commonly abused drugs and describes how they work upon the body. Before discussing specific drugs, it will prove useful to define some of the relevant terms.

> **Tolerance**—A state in which the body's tissue cells become acclimatized to the presence of a drug and fail to respond to ordinarily effective concentrations. Increased quantities of a drug are required to produce the desired effect.

> **Physical dependence**—A state created by the constant administration of a drug in which the presence of the drug in the body is necessary

for normal functioning of the body. If the body is withdrawn, violent physical and psychic reactions occur.

Withdrawal symptoms or **abstinence syndrome** —The reaction occurring in the body when a drug on which the body has acquired dependence is withdrawn.

Psychological dependence—A situation in which one desires and becomes accustomed to a drug but is not physically dependent upon it. Finding and using the drug, however, becomes the main focus in life.

Addiction—A combination of tolerance, psychological and physical dependence

Amphetamines

Amphetamines include three closely related drugs —amphetamine, dextroamphetamine, and methamphetamine. Their street names include: "greenies," "speed," "white crosses," "uppers," "dexies," "bennies," and "crystal." In pure form, they are yellowish crystals that are manufactured in tablet or capsule form. Abusers also sniff the crystals or make a solution and inject it.

Amphetamines increase heart and breathing rates and blood pressure, dilate pupils, and decrease appetite. In addition, the user can experience a dry mouth, sweating, headache, blurred vision, dizziness, sleeplessness, and anxiety. Extremely high doses can cause people to flush or become pale; they can cause a rapid or irregular heartbeat, tremors, loss of coordination, and even physical collapse. An amphetamine injection creates a sudden increase in blood pressure that can cause death from stroke, very high fever, or heart failure.

In addition to the physical effects, users report feeling restless, anxious, and moody. Higher doses intensify the effects, and the user can become excited and talkative and have a false sense of self-confidence and power.

People who use large amounts of amphetamines over a long period of time can also develop an amphetamine psychosis: seeing, hearing, and feeling things that do not exist (hallucinations); having irrational thoughts or beliefs (delusions); and feeling as though people are "out to get them" (paranoia). People in this extremely suspicious state frequently exhibit bizarre—and sometimes violent—behavior. These symptoms usually disappear when people stop using the drug.

Long-term heavy use of amphetamines can lead to malnutrition, skin disorders, ulcers, and various diseases that come from vitamin deficiencies. Lack of sleep, weight loss, and depression also result from regular use. Frequent use of large amounts of amphetamines can produce brain damage that results in speech and thought disturbances. In addition, users who inject amphetamines intravenously can get serious and life-threatening infections from non-sterile equipment or self-prepared solutions that are contaminated. Injecting them can cause lung or heart disease and other diseases of the blood vessels, which can be fatal. Kidney damage, stroke, or other tissue damage also may occur.

Some people report a psychological dependence developing from the use of amphetamines. These users frequently continue to use amphetamines to avoid the "down" mood they get when the drug's effects wear off. In addition, people who use amphetamines may regularly develop tolerance.

When people stop using amphetamines abruptly, they may experience fatigue, long periods of sleep, irritability, hunger, and depression. The length and severity of the depression seem to be related to how much and how often the amphetamines are used.

Look-Alikes

Look-alike stimulants are drugs manufactured to look like real amphetamines and mimic their effects. The drugs usually contain varying amounts of caffeine, ephedrine, and phenylpropanolamine. These three legal substances are weak stimu-

A home cooker for illicit drugs. Sometimes the impurities are more toxic than the drugs.

lants and are often found in over-the-counter preparations, such as diet pills and decongestants. More recently, new drugs called "act-alikes" have been manufactured to avoid new state laws that prohibit look-alikes. The act-alikes contain the same ingredients as the look-alikes, but they don't physically resemble any prescription or over-the-counter drugs. These drugs are sold on the street as "speed" and "uppers" and are expensive, even though they are not as strong as amphetamines. They often are sold to young people, who are told they are legal, safe, and harmless. This is one reason they are being increasingly abused.

Some negative effects of look-alikes, especially when taken in large quantities, are similar to the effects of amphetamines. These effects include anxiety, restlessness, weakness, throbbing headache, difficulty in breathing, and a rapid heartbeat. There have been several reports of severe high blood pressure, leading to cerebral hemorrhaging and death. Often, in an emergency, look-alike drug overdose cases are misidentified by physicians and poison-control centers. This can cause a problem in determining the proper treatment.

One of the greatest dangers is that these drugs are easily available and are being used by young people and others who do not normally abuse drugs. Once people start using these drugs, they may be at high risk for using other drugs.

Because look-alikes are not as strong as real amphetamines, they are extremely dangerous for people who—deliberately or accidentally—take the same amount of real amphetamines as they would take of the look-alikes. For example, people who buy look-alikes on the "street" may, unknowingly, buy real amphetamines and take enough to cause an overdose. On the other hand, people who have abused amphetamines may underestimate the potency of the look-alike drugs and take excessive amounts that can result in a toxic reaction.

Cocaine

Cocaine is a drug extracted from the leaves of the coca plant, which grows in South America. Like the amphetamines, it is a central nervous system stimulant. Cocaine appears in several different forms. Cocaine hydrochloride is the most available form of the drug and is used medically as a local anesthetic. It is usually a fine white crystal-like powder, although at times it comes in larger pieces, which on the "street," are called "rocks." Cocaine is usually sniffed or snorted into the nose, although some users inject it or smoke a form of the drug called freebase.

Another form of the drug is coca paste. It is a crude product smoked in South America. It may be especially dangerous because it also consists of contaminants, such as kerosene, which can cause lung damage.

When cocaine is snorted, the effects begin within a few minutes, peak within fifteen to twenty minutes, and disappear within an hour. These effects include dilated pupils and increased blood pressure, heart rate, breathing rate, and body temperature. The user may have a sense of well-being and feel more energetic or alert, and less hungry.

Freebase is a form of cocaine made by chemically converting "street" cocaine hydrochloride to a purified, altered substance that is more suitable for smoking. Smoking freebase produces a shorter and more intense "high" than most other ways of using the drug because smoking is the most direct and rapid way to get the drug to the brain. Because larger amounts are getting to the brain more quickly, smoking also increases the risks associated with using the drug. These risks include confusion, slurred speech, anxiety, and serious psychological problems.

The dangers of cocaine use vary, depending on how the drug is taken, the dose, and the individual. Some regular users report feelings of restlessness, irritability, anxiety, and sleeplessness. In some people, even low doses of cocaine may create psychological problems. People who use high doses of cocaine over a long period of time may become paranoid or experience what is called "a cocaine psychosis." This may include hallucinations of touch, sight, taste, or smell.

Occasional use can cause a stuffy or runny nose, while chronic snorting can ulcerate the mucous membrane of the nose. Injecting cocaine with unsterile equipment can cause hepatitis, AIDS, or other infections. Furthermore, because preparation of freebase involves the use of volatile solvents, deaths and serious injuries from fire or explosion can occur. Comedian Richard Pryor almost killed himself while freebasing. Overdose deaths can occur when the drug is injected, smoked, or even snorted. Deaths are a result of multiple seizures, while feeling good or high, followed by respiratory and cardiac arrest.

Cocaine is a very dangerous, dependence-producing drug. People use cocaine repeatedly because they like its effects. They get to the point of centering their lives around seeking and using the drug. Smoking freebase increases this risk of dependence. Sometimes people who have been using cocaine over a period of time continue its use in order to avoid depression and fatigue they would feel if they stopped using the drug.

For a while, the growing demand for cocaine and its high price led to the widespread use of substitute drugs that resemble cocaine and may have stimulant effects. Cocaine look-alikes contain ingredients that are legal and that also appear as impurities in samples of street cocaine. Substances that are used to "cut," or dilute, cocaine include household items such as flour, baking soda, talc, sugar, and even rat poison. Local anesthetics, caffeine, and other chemicals also are sold as substitutes. Research on animals, as well as autopsies performed on humans, determined that impurities in cocaine can cause almost as many problems as the drug itself.

Crack

Crack is the cheapest and most intensely addictive form of cocaine. The drug produces a fifteen-minute high within ten seconds of being smoked. Its users can become addicted within days and are inclined then to become hyperactive, paranoid, and highly dangerous. Compared with other forms of cocaine, a hit of this drug appears to be cheap. At $10 a vial, the drug is literally and financially within the reach of even

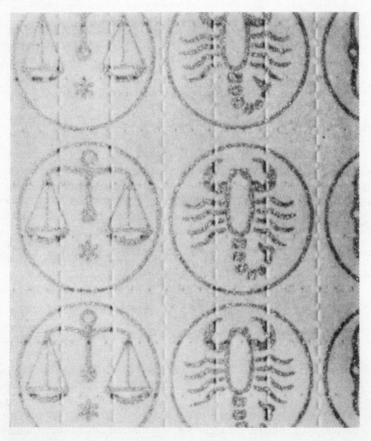

Blotter Acid. Almost a thing of the past? LSD use is down fifty percent in the last five years.

grade-school children. No longer is cocaine just a plaything for the rich and famous. Crack is the fast-food version of the drug, cheap to buy and profitable to sell, the dealer's dream that becomes the user's nightmare. How callous these drug lords are with their deliberate marketing strategy to hook younger kids, in ripe inner-city communities, the best place to spread an initially inexpensive product. Even crack's supposed cheapness is a myth. At $10 a gram, it's approximately twice as expensive as a similar amount of cocaine powder. It's simply packaged as a bargain.

I first became aware of crack in 1985 when Robert Stutman of DEA showed me a few vials of it and predicted it would become the nation's fastest growing drug of choice. His forecast has proven correct, especially for New York. I've seen the crack trade in the city develop to where it's now available from 500 to 700 crack houses.

Opiates

Opiates, sometimes referred to as narcotics, are a group of drugs that are used medically to relieve pain, but also have a high potential for abuse. Some opiates come from a resin taken from the seed pod of the Asian poppy. This group of drugs includes opium, morphine, heroin, and codeine. Other opiates, such as meperidine (Demerol), are synthesized or manufactured.

Opium appears as dark brown chunks or as a powder and is usually smoked or eaten. Heroin can be a white or brownish powder that is usually dissolved in water and then injected. Most street preparations of heroin are diluted, or "cut," with other substances such as sugar or quinine. Other opiates come in a variety of forms including capsules, tablets, syrups, solutions, and suppositories.

Heroin ("junk," "smack") accounts for ninety percent of the opiate abuse in the United States. Sometimes opiates with legal medicinal uses also are abused. These include morphine, meperidine, paregoric (which contains opium), and cough syrups containing codeine.

Opiates tend to relax the user. When opiates are injected, the user feels an immediate "rush." Other initial and unpleasant effects include restlessness, nausea, and vomiting. The user may go "on the nod," going back and forth from feeling alert to drowsy. With very large doses, the user cannot be awakened, pupils become smaller, and the skin becomes cold, moist, and bluish in color. Breathing slows and death may occur.

Dependence is likely, especially if a person uses a lot of the drug or even uses it occasionally over a long period of time. Tolerance also develops.

The physical dangers depend on the specific opiate used, its source, the dose, and the way it is used. Most of the dangers are caused by using too much of a drug, the use of unsterile needles, contamination of the drug itself, or combining the drug with other substances. Over time, opiate users may develop infections of the heart lining and valves, skin abscesses, and congested lungs. Infections from unsterile solutions, syringes, and needles can cause illnesses such as liver disease, tetanus, and serum hepatitis.

Researchers estimate that nearly half the women who are dependent on opiates suffer anemia, heart disease, diabetes, pneumonia, or hepatitis during pregnancy and childbirth. They have more spontaneous abortions, breech deliveries, Caesarean sections, premature births, and stillbirths. Infants born to these women often have withdrawal symptoms that may last several weeks or months. Many of these babies die.

When an opiate-dependent person stops taking the drug, withdrawal usually begins within four to six hours after the last dose. Withdrawal symptoms include uneasiness, diarrhea, abdominal cramps, chills, sweating, nausea, and runny nose and eyes. The intensity of these symptoms depends on how much of the drug was taken, how often, and for how long. Withdrawal symptoms for most opiates are strong for approximately twenty-four to seventy-two hours after they begin and subside with seven to ten days. Sometimes symptoms such as sleeplessness and drug craving can last for months.

Sedative-Hypnotics

Sedative-hypnotics are drugs that depress or slow down the body's functions. Often these drugs are referred to as tranquilizers, sleeping pills, or sedatives. Their effects range from calming anxious people to promoting sleep. Both tranquilizers and sleeping pills can have either effect, depending on how much is taken. At high doses, or when they are abused, many of these drugs can cause unconsciousness and death.

Barbiturates and benzodiazepines are the two major categories of sedative-hypnotics. The drugs in each of these groups are similar in chemical structure. Sedative-hypnotics can cause both physical and psychological dependence. Regular use over a long period of time may result in tolerance. When regular users suddenly stop using large doses of these drugs, they may develop physical withdrawal symptoms ranging from restlessness, insomnia, and anxiety to convulsions and death.

Taken together, alcohol and sedative-hypnotics can kill. The use of barbiturates and other sedative-hypnotics with other drugs that slow down the body, such as alcohol, multiplies their effects and greatly increases the risk of death. Overdose deaths can occur when barbiturates and alcohol are used together, either deliberately or accidentally.

Babies born to mothers who abuse sedatives during their pregnancies may be physically dependent on the drugs and show withdrawals symptoms shortly after birth. Their symptoms may include breathing problems, feeding difficulties, disturbed sleep, sweating, irritability, and fever. Many sedative-hypnotics pass easily through the placenta and have caused birth defects and behavioral problems in babies born to women who have abused these drugs during their pregnancies.

Barbiturates

Barbiturates are often called "barbs" and "downers." Barbiturates that are commonly abused include amobarbital

(Amytal), pentobarbital (Nembutal), and secobarbital (Seconal). These drugs are sold in capsules and tablets or sometimes appear in a liquid form or suppositories.

The effects of barbiturates are, in many ways, similar to the effects of alcohol. Small amounts produce calmness and relax muscles. Somewhat larger doses can cause slurred speech, staggering gait, poor judgment, and slow, uncertain reflexes. These effects make it dangerous to drive a car or operate machinery. Large doses can cause unconsciousness and death.

Barbiturate overdose is a factor in nearly one-third of all reported drug-related deaths. These include suicides and accidental drug poisonings. Accidental deaths sometimes occur when a user takes one dose, becomes confused, and unintentionally takes additional or larger doses. With barbiturates there is less difference between the amount that produces sleep and the amount that kills. Furthermore, barbiturate withdrawal can be more serious than heroin withdrawal.

Other Sedative-Hypnotics

All other sedative-hypnotics can be abused, including benzodiazepines. Diazepam (Valium), chlordiazepoxide (Librium), and chlorazepate (Tranxene) are examples of benzodiazepines. These drugs are also sold on the street as downers. As with barbiturates, tolerance and dependence can develop if benzodiazepines are taken regularly in high doses over prolonged periods of time.

Other sedative-hypnotics that are abused include glutethimide (Doriden), ethchlorvynol (Placidyl), and methaqualone (Sopor, Quāālude).

Methaqualone ("Sopors," "ludes") was originally prescribed to reduce anxiety during the day and as a sleeping aid. It is one of the most commonly abused drugs and can cause both physical and psychological dependence. The dangers from abusing methaqualone include injury or death from car accidents caused by faulty judgment and drowsiness, convulsions, coma, and death from overdose.

As with stimulants, there are pills manufactured to look like real sedative-hypnotics and mimic their effects. Sometimes look-alikes contain over-the-counter drugs such as antihistamines and decongestants, which tend to cause drowsiness. The negative effects can include nausea, stomach cramps, lack of coordination, temporary memory loss, becoming out of touch with the surroundings, and anxious behavior.

Hallucinogens

Hallucinogens, or psychedelics, are drugs that affect a person's perceptions, sensations, thinking, self-awareness, and emotions. Hallucinogens include drugs such as LSD, mescaline, psilocybin, and DMT. Some hallucinogens come from natural sources, such as mescaline, which comes from the peyote cactus. Others, such as LSD, are synthetic or manufactured.

PCP is sometimes considered a hallucinogen because it has some of the same effects. However, it does not fit easily into any one drug category because it also can relieve pain or act as a stimulant.

LSD is manufactured from lysergic acid, which is found in ergot, a fungus that grows on rye and other grains. LSD was discovered in 1938 and is one of the most potent mood-changing chemicals. It is odorless, colorless, and tasteless. LSD is sold on the street in tablets, capsules, or occasionally in liquid form. It is usually taken by mouth, but sometimes it is injected. Often LSD is added to absorbent paper, such as blotter paper, then divided into small decorated squares, with each square representing one dose.

Mescaline comes from peyote cactus, and although it is not as strong as LSD, its effects are similar. Mescaline is usually smoked or swallowed in the form of capsules or tablets.

Psilocybin comes from certain mushrooms. It is sold in tablet or capsule form so it can be swallowed. The mushrooms themselves, fresh or dried, may be eaten. DMT is another psychedelic drug that acts like LSD. Its effects begin almost immediately and last between thirty and sixty minutes.

The effects of psychedelics are unpredictable. It depends on the amount taken, the user's personality, mood, and expectations, and the surroundings in which the drug is used. The user generally feels the first effects of the drug thirty to ninety minutes after taking it. The physical effects include dilated pupils, higher body temperature, increased heart rate and blood pressure, sweating, loss of appetite, sleeplessness, dry mouth, and tremors.

Sensations and feelings change, too. The user may feel several different emotions at once or swing rapidly from one emotion to another. The person's sense of time and self changes. Sensations may seem to "cross over," giving the user the feeling of "hearing" colors and "seeing" sounds. All of these changes can be frightening and can cause panic.

Having a bad psychological reaction to LSD and similar drugs is common. The scary sensations may lasts a few minutes or several hours and be mildly frightening or terrifying. The user may experience panic, confusion, suspiciousness, anxiety, feelings of helplessness, and loss of control. Sometimes taking a hallucinogen such as LSD can unmask mental or emotional problems that were previously unknown to the user. Flashbacks, in which the person experiences a drug's effects without having to take the drug again, can occur.

Research has shown some changes in the mental functions of heavy users of LSD, but they are not present in all cases. Heavy users sometimes develop signs of organic brain damage, such as impaired memory and attention span, mental confusion, and difficulty with abstract thinking. These signs may be strong or they may be subtle. It is not yet known whether such mental changes are permanent or if they disappear when LSD use is stopped.

PCP

PCP (phencyclidine) is most often called "angel dust." It was first developed as an anesthetic in the 1950s. However, it was taken off the market for human use because it sometimes caused hallucinations.

PCP is available in a number of forms. It can be a pure, white crystal-like powder, or a tablet or capsule. It can be swallowed, smoked, sniffed, or injected. PCP is sometimes sprinkled on marijuana or parsley and smoked.

Although PCP is illegal, it is easily manufactured. It is often sold as mescaline, THC, or other drugs. Sometimes it may not even be PCP, but a lethal by-product of the drug. Users can never be sure what they are buying since it is manufactured illegally.

Effects depend on how much is taken, the way it is used, and the individual. Effects include increased heart rate and blood pressure, flushing, sweating, dizziness, and numbness. When large doses are taken, effects include drowsiness, convulsions, and coma. Taking large amounts of PCP can also cause death from repeated convulsions, heart and lung failure, or ruptured blood vessels in the brain.

Users find it difficult to describe or predict the effects of the drug. For some users, PCP in small amounts acts as a stimulant, speeding up body functions. For many users, PCP changes how users perceive their own bodies and things around them. Speech, muscle coordination, and vision are affected; senses of touch and pain are dulled; and body movements are slowed. Time seems to "space out."

PCP can produce violent or bizarre behavior in people who are not normally that way. This behavior can lead to death from drownings, burns, falls, and automobile accidents. Regular PCP use affects memory, perception, concentration, and judgment. Users may show signs of paranoia, fearfulness, and anxiety. During these times, some users may become aggressive, while others may withdraw and have difficulty communicating. A temporary mental disturbance, or a disturbance of the user's thought processes (a PCP psychosis), may last for days or weeks. Long-term PCP users report memory and speech difficulties, as well as hearing voices or sounds that do not exist.

Inhalants

Inhalants are breathable chemicals that produce psychoactive (mind-altering) vapors. People do not usually think of inhalants as drugs because most were never meant to be used in that way. These include solvents, aerosols, some anesthetics, and other chemicals. Examples are model airplane glue, nail polish remover, lighter and cleaning fluids, and gasoline. Aerosols that are used as inhalants include paints, cookware-coating agents, hair sprays, and other spray products. Anesthetics include halothane and nitrous oxide (laughing gas). Amyl nitrite and butyl nitrite are inhalants that also are abused.

Amyl nitrite is a clear, yellowish liquid that is sold in a cloth-covered, sealed bulb, often in head shops or sex shops. When the bulb is broken it makes a snapping sound; thus, they are nicknamed "snappers" or "poppers." Amyl nitrite is used for heart patients and for diagnostic purposes because it dilates blood vessels and makes the heart beat faster. Reports of amyl nitrite abuse occurred before 1979, when it was available without a prescription. When it became available by prescription only, many users abused butyl nitrite instead.

Butyl nitrite is packaged in small bottles and sold under a variety of trade names, such as Locker Room and Rush. It produces a high that lasts from a few seconds to several minutes. The immediate effects include decreased blood pressure, followed by an increased heart rate, flushed face and neck, dizziness, and headache.

Young people, especially between the ages of seven and seventeen, are more likely to abuse inhalants, partly because they are readily available and inexpensive. Sometimes children unintentionally misuse inhalant products that are often found around the house. Parents should make sure that these substances, like medicines, are kept away from young children.

Although different in makeup, nearly all of the abused inhalants produce effects similar to anesthetics, which act to slow down the body's functions. At low doses, users may feel slightly stimulated; at higher amounts, they may feel less inhibited, less in control; at high doses, a user can lose consciousness.

Initial effects include nausea, sneezing, coughing, nosebleeds, feeling and looking tired, bad breath, lack of coordination, and loss of appetite. Solvents and aerosols also decrease the heart and breathing rate and affect judgment.

How strong these effects are depends on the experience and personality of the user, how much is taken, the specific substance inhaled, and the user's surroundings. The high from inhalants tends to be short but can last several hours if used repeatedly.

Deep breathing of the vapors, or prolonged use over a short period of time, may result in losing touch with one's surroundings, a loss of self-control, violent behavior, unconsciousness, or death. Using inhalants can cause nausea and vomiting. If a person is unconscious when vomiting occurs, death can result from asphyxiation.

Sniffing highly concentrated amounts of solvents or aerosol sprays can produce heart failure and instant death. Sniffing can cause death the first time or at any time during and after use. High concentrations of inhalants cause death from suffocation by displacing the oxygen in the lungs. Inhalants also can cause death by depressing the central nervous system so much that breathing slows down until it stops.

Death from inhalants is usually caused by a very high concentration of inhalant fumes. Deliberately inhaling from a paper bag greatly increases the chance of suffocation. Even when using aerosols or volative (vaporous) products for their legitimate purposes—that is, painting, cleaning, and the like—it is wise to do so in a well-ventilated room or outdoors.

Long-term use can cause weight loss, fatigue, electrolyte imbalance, and muscle fatigue. Repeated sniffing of concentrated vapors over a number of years can cause permanent damage to the nervous system, which means greatly reduced physical and mental capabilities. In addition, long-term sniffing of certain inhalants can damage the liver, kidneys, blood, and bone marrow. Tolerance is likely to develop from most inhalants when they are used regularly.

As in all drug use, taking more than one drug at a time multiplies the risks. Using inhalants while taking other drugs that slow down the body's functions, such as tranquilizers, sleeping pills, or alcohol, increases the risk of death from overdose. Loss of consciousness, coma, or death can result.

Marijuana

Marijuana (grass, pot, reefer, weed) is the common name for a crude drug made from the plant *Cannabis sativa*. The main mind-altering (psychoactive) ingredient in marijuana is THC (delta-9-tetrahydrocannabinol), but more than 400 other chemicals also are contained in the plant. A marijuana "joint" (cigarette) is made from the dried particles of the plant. The amount of THC in the marijuana determines how strong its effects will be.

The type of plant, the weather, the soil, the time of harvest, and other factors determine the strength of marijuana. The strength of today's marijuana is as much as ten times greater than marijuana used in the early 1970s. This more potent marijuana increases physical and mental effects and the possibility of health problems for the user.

Hashish, or hash, is made by taking the resin from the leaves and flowers of the marijuana plant and pressing it into cakes or slabs. Hash is usually stronger than crude marijuana and may contain five to ten times as much THC. Hash oil may contain up to fifty percent THC. Pure THC is almost never available, except for research. Substances sold as THC on the street often turn out to be something else, such as PCP.

Some immediate physical effects of marijuana include a faster heartbeat and pulse rate, bloodshot eyes, and a dry mouth and throat. No scientific evidence indicates that marijuana improves hearing, eyesight, and skin sensitivity.

Studies on marijuana's mental effects show that the drug can impair or reduce short-term memory, alter one's sense of time, and reduce the ability to do things requiring concentration, swift reactions, and coordination, such as driving a car or operating machinery.

A common adverse reaction to marijuana is the "acute panic anxiety reaction." People describe this reaction as an extreme fear of "losing control," which causes panic. The symptoms usually disappear in a few hours.

Long-term regular users of marijuana may become psychologically dependent. They may have a difficult time limiting their use, they may need more of the drug to get the same effect, and they may develop problems with their jobs and interpersonal relationships. The drug can become the most important aspect of their lives.

One major concern about marijuana is its possible effects on young people as they grow up. Research shows that the earlier people start using drugs, the more likely they are to go on to experiment with other drugs. In addition, when young people start using marijuana regularly, they often lose interest and are not motivated to do schoolwork. The effects of marijuana can interfere with learning by impairing thinking, reading comprehension, and verbal and mathematical skills. Research shows that students do not remember what they have learned when they are high.

Driving experiments show that marijuana affects a wide range of skills needed for safe driving—thinking and reflexes are slowed, making it hard for drivers to respond to sudden, unexpected events. Also, a driver's ability to "track" (stay in lane) through curves, to brake quickly, and to maintain speed and the proper distance between cars is affected. Research shows that these skills are impaired for at least four to six hours after smoking a single marijuana cigarette, long after the high is gone. If a person drinks alcohol, together with using marijuana, the risk of an accident increases greatly. Marijuana presents a definite danger on the road and in the sky. Studies show that airline pilots on a simulator twenty-four hours after marijuana use cannot land a plane safely.

Some studies suggest that the use of marijuana during pregnancy may result in premature babies and in low birth weights. Other studies of men and women who use marijuana have shown that marijuana may influence levels of some hormones relating to sexuality. Women may have irregular menstrual cycles, and both men and women may have a temporary loss of fertility. These findings suggest that marijuana may be especially harmful during adolescence, a period of rapid physical and sexual development.

Marijuana use increases the heart rate as much as fifty percent, depending on the amount of THC in the cigarette. It can cause chest pain in people who have a poor blood supply to the heart—and it produces these effects more rapidly than does tobacco smoke.

Scientists believe that marijuana can be especially harmful to the lungs because users often inhale the unfiltered smoke deeply and hold it in their lungs as long as possible. Therefore, the smoke is in contact with lung tissues for longer periods of time, which irritates the lungs and damages the way they function. Marijuana smoke contains some of the same ingredients found in tobacco smoke that can cause emphysema and cancer. In addition, many marijuana users also smoke cigarettes; the combined effects of smoking these two substances create an increased health risk.

Marijuana smoke has been found to contain more cancer-causing agents than is found in tobacco smoke. Examination of human lung tissue that had been exposed to marijuana smoke over a long period of time in laboratory tests showed cellular changes called metaplasia that are considered precancerous. In laboratory tests, the tars from marijuana smoke have produced tumors when applied to animal skin. These studies suggest that it is likely that marijuana may cause cancer if used for a number of years.

"Burnout" is a term used by marijuana smokers to describe the effect of prolonged use. Young people who smoke marijuana heavily over long periods of time can become dull, slow-moving, and inattentive. These burned-out users are sometimes so unaware of their surroundings that they do not respond when friends speak to them, and they do not realize they have a problem.

When marijuana is smoked, THC, its active ingredient, is absorbed by most tissues and organs in the body; however, it is primarily found in fat tissues. The body, in its attempt to rid itself of the foreign chemical, chemically transforms the THC into metabolites. Urine tests can detect THC for up to a week after people have smoked marijuana (far longer for chronic users). Tests involving radioactively labeled THC have traced metabolites in animals for up to a month.

Designer Drugs

High technology has entered the world of drugs as new "designer drugs" are being synthesized in underground laboratories. These drugs represent a high level of sophistication and are twenty to three thousand times more powerful than heroin. Until last year, because they varied slightly in chemical composition from already controlled substances, they were not even illegal. To date, designer drugs have remained primarily on the West Coast, but it would seem only a matter of time before they spread across the nation.

Summing Up

Today, all people are making a grave mistake if they think they are smart enough to administer the proper amount of a drug for themselves because of all the intangibles: individual tolerance, dubious street certification or approval, impurities due to development or treatment of products in a makeshift laboratory, made in a clandestine manner. I wonder if drug users have a real understanding or confidence in what they are ingesting or if they really care. Drug use is a shortcut to self-destruction. I'm afraid for some thrill seekers, danger is attractive.

6. RECENT DEVELOPMENTS

RESEARCH

I must preface my remarks about research on drug abuse by saying that it is in a stage of infancy. Our first real understanding of how drugs interact with the brain dates from the 1950s. We didn't establish a federal agency, the National Institute on Drug Abuse (NIDA), to monitor drug use and sponsor research until the early 1970s. An additional problem is that the drug scene is constantly changing. The PCP problem in this country, for example, hit us quickly, and by the time research on the drug was beginning to reach conclusions, the epidemic had subsided.

Another factor complicating research into drug use among youth is how recent widespread use in this age group actually is. While we have centuries of at least anecdotal evidence regarding adults and drugs, large numbers of young people did not begin abusing drugs until the 1960s. When I was growing up, the quality and quantity of drugs was low. I wasn't even aware of their availability until I was in high school. A recent *Weekly Reader* survey of 500,000 grade-school children found that one-quarter of them had already felt pressure to try drugs. Within one generation, the user population has changed dramatically.

Some of the limitations of research apply to both youths and adults. The full consequences of a particular drug's use are revealed only after a sufficiently large percent of the population has used the substance for a sufficiently long period of time. Reliable studies of marijuana were not really available until this decade. Drug experiments performed on animals are always subject to the variables of differences between species. Most abusers use several drugs, and it is generally impossible to determine the quality or quantity of the drug used and, in some cases, even the drug's true identity.

Despite these handicaps, considerable progress has been made in advancing our frontiers of knowledge about drugs. The most important recent discoveries, those regarding the physiology of pleasure, were sketched in the chapter "Understanding Addiction." These original discoveries, first applied only to drug abuse, have now proven valuable in studying depression, insanity, and eating disorders. All appear to be different facets of the same problem. Using our new found knowledge of molecular psychology, we are beginning to unlock some of the mysteries and secrets of the mind.

The most recent annual national survey of drug abuse among high school seniors, the prime group for studying drug use trends, also gives reason for optimism. The National Institute on Drug Abuse sponsors the survey which has been conducted by the University of Michigan's Institute for Social Research since 1975. The good news is that the downward trend in illicit drug use, which stalled in 1985, continued to decline in 1986. The number of high school seniors indicating any drug use fell from sixty-one percent to fifty-eight percent. Those using drugs within the last month declined from thirty percent to twenty-seven percent. Marijuana users fell to twenty-three percent from twenty-six percent—continuing a six year downward trend. Even more dramatic is the trend of daily marijuana users which declined another percent to four percent (down from eleven percent in 1978!) Significant declines were also noted in amphetamines and methaqualone. Use of hallucinogens was unchanged but low, 11%, a drop of nearly half from 1982 (twenty-one percent).

The bad news in the survey is that overall drug use by American youth is unacceptably high and despite increased public attention to its dangers, cocaine use stayed at the same level, seventeen percent. Six percent of the class of 1986 had used cocaine in the prior month. The survey also measured

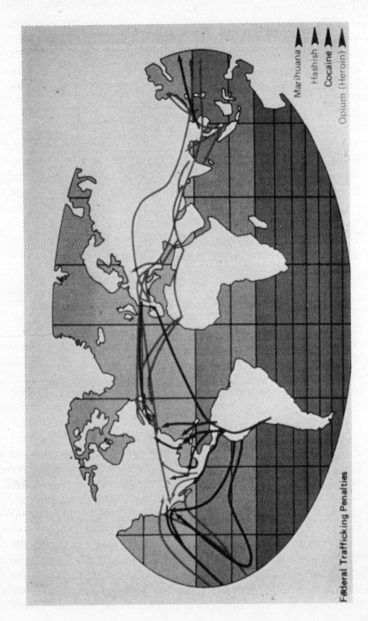

Federal Trafficking Penalties

Marihuana
Hashish
Cocaine
Opium (Heroin)

How drugs get to us.

crack use for the first time with four percent reporting use. About half of the schools indicated some crack use which shows that the drug has spread and is not confined to just a few large cities. It should be noted that the 1986 survey was conducted before the deaths of Len Bias and Don Rogers and I hope these events will have an impact that can be measured this year.

There was little change in alcohol or heroin consumption and only a slight decline in cigarette smoking, surprising because society seems to be slowly turning away from tobacco. Clearly we still have a lot of work to do. We still have the highest rate of youth drug abuse in the world, but the slow decline in overall drug use is encouraging.

EDUCATION/PREVENTION

To the surprise of many, drug-education programs are not a recent development. By the 1890s almost every state in the Union required instruction on the evils of alcohol and narcotics. In California schools, for example, all classes in all grades received instruction. While it is true that drug-education programs increase knowledge about drugs, until recently there has been no indication that the programs changed attitudes or altered behavior. Programs based on moralizing or terrorizing are the least effective. There seems to me to be a serious question raised by employing adult ex-users in prevention programs. Some efforts have apparently even stimulated greater drug experimentation and use. In 1973 the National Commission on Drug Abuse recommended a moratorium on drug-education programs in the schools, at least until the existing programs could be evaluated.

Traditionally, substance abuse prevention programs have focused on factual information regarding the dangers involved. If students knew the hazards, it was reasoned they wouldn't use drugs. Rational decisions to abstain would result from presentations by physicians, law enforcement officials, educators, and often, ex-users. Fear arousal was frequently employed. The available evidence suggests that this method

Confiscated marijuana soon to go up in smoke.

has not yet worked in preventing or altering drug abuse.

Another approach to prevention involves what is called "affective" education. Self-esteem, decision-making, and social development are stressed. One basis for this technique is the thought that drugs provide a mirage of well-being to young people who have not yet acquired the skills and values that make real life rewarding. These curricula and other forums concentrate on developing skills and values. Conflict management, dispute resolution, decision-making, risk assessment, coping skills, dealing with peer pressure, and accepting family and individual responsibilities put drug education into a larger context.

Within the last few years, however, new prevention techniques have emerged that show increasing promise to actually alter substance abuse patterns. These new techniques borrow from "affective" education, but add a new dimension: focusing on social influences that encourage substance abuse. Students are taught about how social pressures to smoke will affect them, and their mistaken notions about smoking ("Everybody does it") are corrected. They are helped to construct arguments against smoking and are "innoculated" against the pressure to smoke by being subjected to increasingly strong pro-smoking messages. Over a dozen studies show this approach has succeeded at least in delaying the onset of smoking. Programs that teach youth how to resist social pressures to try drugs seem the most effective. Studies conducted by the Institute of Prevention Research at the University of Southern California found that curricula that built social-resistance skills reduced the number of students who experimented with drugs by fifty percent. Even if experimentation is only delayed, the chances of becoming a regular user are lowered.

Another avenue that appears promising focuses on health and appearance. A recent National Collegiate Athletic Association study indicates that athletes are far more motivated by health concerns than by sanctions or rules prohibiting drug use. And appearance conscious adolescents seem to be sensitive to the short-term effects of drug use—bloodshot eyes, discolored teeth, less concern for hygiene. A 1984 report by the Rand Corporation recommends that anti-drug education borrow techniques from successful anti-smoking programs. These campaigns stress not long-term health effects, which are too far in the future to impress youth, but immediate results of smoking, such as bad breath.

These developments in prevention education give me hope that we're finally on the right path. I also wish to affirm my belief that many basic deterrents to drug use are not directly connected with drugs: interest and participation in school activities; alternatives within the home and community; regional and national action on youth issues. The list could go on at length. People take drugs to feel better, relieve pain, reward themselves, alter states of mind, and to be part of a peer group, among other reasons. If the alternatives to drug use can satisfy the needs that drugs appear to fill, they become appropriate options.

TREATMENT

Recent discoveries are effecting major changes in treatment programs. A growing number of the therapeutic community now view addiction as a physiological disease that can be overcome, rather than a moral disease with an unacceptably high incidence of failed treatment. Research into the neuro-mechanics of brain cells has produced new drug therapies to control withdrawal and craving symptoms. Clonidine is one such drug. It is a non-addicting, non-opiate like drug that relieves opiate withdrawal. It may also relieve nicotine withdrawal. Another new drug, Naltrexone, assists in relapse prevention for opium addicts. Recently approved by the Food and Drug Administration, the drug blocks the effects of opium. It is a perfect neutralizing agent in that it works against all opiates, is long acting, and is non-addictive. It is particularly popular with recovering medical professionals who face the constant temptation of access to drugs in their workplace.

Non-drug therapies that stimulate the body's own endorphin production are also proving effective. One such technique is called transcutaneous electrical neural stimulation (TENS). A small device worn on the patient's belt emits a current carried by electrodes to the patient's scalp and induces the brain to produce endorphins. Acupuncture also produces these key hormones. When combined with yoga and meditation, this is proving successful in a California program treating heroin addicts. A huge advantage of such procedures is that they can be performed on an outpatient basis, greatly reducing cost and allowing the addict to maintain a life outside the clinic.

Other non-drug therapies have been developed in the last few years that work. One behavioral approach is contingency contracting. The addict-patient and therapist agree to a contract specifically designating expected behavior. For example, a lawyer-addict may be required to submit a letter identifying himself as an addict and informing the bar association that relapse has occured and suspension from practice should follow. In the case that the addict fails a drug test during treatment, the letter is mailed. With so much to lose, this technique provides tremendous incentive, particularly for professionals such as attorneys and physicians, to remain drug free.

These new treatment programs are significant changes from traditional approaches that break down the patient's "addictive" personality so that a new one can be built. Instead, patients are told they suffer from a disease that gives them a sick personality, not the other way around. Like diabetes, addiction is not the patient's fault. If not treated, it is incurable, progressive, and usually fatal. As with diabetics, if addicts wish to live, they must change their life-style and obtain treatment and abstain, not from sugar, but from drugs. Making patients responsible for their treatment—but not their addiction—helps restore the lost self-esteem that seems an inevitable result of addiction.

The new therapies place great emphasis on total and lifelong abstinence from *all* drugs. Even if the drug used is different from the drug for which the patient originally sought treatment, the chances are high that use of any psychoactive drug will lead the patient back to his or her drug of choice.

Self-help peer groups can help the individual achieve abstinence. Peer counseling seems particularly useful in treating young addicts. Frequently it is one's peers who get young people started using drugs, and peers appear effective in getting youths to stop using drugs. In contrast with earlier drug-treatment programs that had such high rates of failure, several of the new therapies can boast success rates of up to sixty-five percent. I should stress, however, that these figures are often based on follow-up surveys done six months to a year after treatment. To really get a handle on how successful treatment is, we must study former users several years after treatment.

Alcoholics Anonymous

Few organizations have had as much success as Alcoholics Anonymous (AA) in modifying behavior of addicts. Their road to recovery is frequently emulated by other drug-therapy programs, and such non-drug programs as Gamblers Anonymous and Overeaters Anonymous. Moving from addiction to control consists of several stages.

The Twelve Steps of Alcoholics Anonymous

1. We admitted we were powerless over alcohol —that our lives had become unmanageable.
2. Came to believe that a Power greater than ourselves could restore us to sanity.
3. Made a decision to turn our will and our lives over to the care of God *as we understood Him.*
4. Made a searching and fearless moral inventory of ourselves.
5. Admitted to God, to ourselves, and to another human being the exact nature of our wrongs.
6. Were entirely ready to have God remove all these defects of character.
7. Humbly asked Him to remove our shortcomings.
8. Made a list of all persons we had harmed, and became willing to make amends to them all.

9. Made direct amends to such people wherever possible, except when to do so would injure them or others.
10. Continued to take personal inventory and when we were wrong promptly admitted it.
11. Sought through prayer and meditation to improve our conscious contact with God *as we understood Him,* praying only for knowledge of His will for us and the power to carry that out.
12. Having had a spiritual awakening as the result of these steps, we tried to carry this message to alcoholics, and to practice these principles in all our affairs.

The Twelve Steps reprinted with permission of Alcoholics Anonymous World Services, Inc.

While AA was founded in 1935, I include it and its precepts here because it is the foundation for many new treatments. One, in particular I would like to mention, is Operation New Hope in Paso Robles, California. It is directed by Dock Ellis, the former major league pitcher.

ENFORCEMENT

Perhaps the most significant recent development in enforcing drug laws is seizing profits and assets derived from drug trafficking. Since early times forfeiture has been a tool of authorities, but only in the last few years has it been used by the Drug Enforcement Agency (DEA). Last year alone the DEA seized $370 million in drug dealers' assets. Seizures made by state and local enforcement authorities have also risen rapidly. In a recent effort to curtail crack sales, New York police have begun to confiscate the cars of *customers* driving into the city to make their buys. If these trends continue to develop and to be aggressively enforced, forfeitures will be able to pay for an increasingly larger share of enforcement costs. I also hope that the legal and political authorities will apply significant amounts of these profits to education and prevention programs.

The newest recommendation relating to cars and drugs comes from U.S. Secretary of Education William Bennett. He suggests that teen-agers found guilty of possession or other drug offenses temporarily lose the right to drive or apply for driving permits or licenses. Bennett theorizes that the adolescent passion for the automobile will prove stronger than the temptation of drugs.

Another imaginative idea was recently suggested by the New York State Law Enforcement Council. New York has been hard hit by the crack epidemic on top of its already heavy drug traffic. While additions to state and city prisons have been made, the problem overcrowding continues. The lack of jail space makes it difficult to sentence offenders to prison. The council has proposed placing first-time drug offenders in work camps located on the grounds of state prisons. In this way convicts could be imprisoned without taking up cell space. Their sentences would include supervised work, drug counseling, and education. Convicts who meet their obligations could be paroled early. Rehabilitation would be a major goal.

The problems presented to us by enforcement are the most insoluable. Progress in other areas discussed in this chapter give me further hope that the epidemic of drug use in America can be turned around. We cannot win the fight simply through more efficient or even imaginative law enforcement. Cooperation between federal, state, and local authorities has never been higher. The response of foreign governments has increased. The U.S. military is now assisting in intercepting drugs, even to the point of using AWACs observation flights. But as enforcement technology gets more sophisticated, so does smuggling technology. As officials increase their efficiency, so do the drug traffickers. The ultimate answer to cutting drug use in America is not increasing enforcement, but reducing demand.

7. PROMISING PROGRAMS

> *There are countless ways to go wrong, but only a very few ways to go right; hence, our best chance to deal successfully with our contemporary problems and those of the future is to learn from the success stories of our times.*

> —Rene Dubos

As I travel across the country during the baseball season on road trips and during the off season on speaking engagements, I try to keep my eyes open for programs that have established a successful track record in the drug field. Many organizations, learning about the work of the Winfield Foundation, send us materials about their programs. The staff of the foundation, its associates, and volunteers are diligent in bringing promising programs to my attention. I'd like to identify and describe a few of the efforts around the nation that we believe are making a difference.

SUPER TEAMS

Students Unified with Pros Encouraging Responsibility is a unique program concept. It was founded in 1984 by Brig Owen, former defensive captain for the Washington Redskins. The program joins the Washington, D. C. public school system, the Washington, D. C. Commission on Public Health, and the National Football League Players' Association (N.F.L.P.A.) in a massive campaign to prevent drug use among teens in three Washington area public high schools. The N.F.L.P.A. has pledged its support and has committed itself to obtaining a core-group of professional athletes, active and retired, to become members of the SUPER TEAMS training staff and to follow-up activities during the school year

81

by providing motivation to the high school students on a regular basis. This follow-up assures greater success for the program and makes it very different from other ordinary "peer leadership" programs.

The public school system has agreed to cooperate with the SUPER TEAM concept by providing space for the operation of the program. They will work closely with SUPER TEAMS on scheduling the intense training for the ninety students and nine adult advisors in the peer counseling techniques. They will also inform, support, and promote the SUPER TEAM drug prevention message to the student body at each of the three designated Washington, D. C. public high schools.

The Commission on Public Health (C.P.H.) has pledged to provide medical information: pamphlets, books, magazines, and other reading material and lectures, where possible, on the physical, mental and emotional effects which can result from drug and alcohol abuse. C.P.H. will also provide referral information to adult SUPER TEAM advisors when student counselors discover young people at their school who are active drug abusers but wish to discontinue this behavior.

The concept behind SUPER TEAMS is to develop a core group of student leaders and athletes to serve as role models and to serve as counselors in order to affect all students at a particular school. The trained students will also be used to positively influence younger children in their communities.

This program model utilizes the influence of professional athletes from the high school (football, baseball and basketball teams, and the like), other student leaders, school officials, parents, and coaches. The SUPER TEAM effort focuses on those students who are integrally involved in the school sports program—or extra-curricular activities for both male and female, the band, the cheerleaders, and other influential students. Young leaders often have an impact on other students far beyond his or her own perception.

The SUPER TEAM program design consists of three phases. The first is an in-service training seminar specifically for coaches, school counselors, teachers, parents and school administrators. Phase two of the program is a five day residential training seminar for the SUPER TEAM adult advisors and student members. This phase also includes the day-to-day operation of the program within the schools once the residential training is complete. The technical assistants, follow-up and evaluation activities associated with the program constitute phase three of the program.

For more information contact:

> SUPER TEAMS
> 1411 K Street, N.W.
> Suite 910
> Washington, D.C. 20005
> (202) 783-1533

Texans' War on Drugs

Texans' War on Drugs (TWOD), a statewide drug-abuse prevention organization, is federally funded and state-administered. Its goal is to reduce significantly the use of drugs by the young people of Texas by educating and raising the awareness level of the public. TWOD is the action arm of the Texans' War on Drugs Committee, chaired by Texas businessman H. Ross Perot as an appointee of the governor of Texas.

Headquartered in Austin, TWOD has regional field offices thoughout the state. Each office is headed by a regional field coordinator who provides information, education, and technical assistance to the public. In addition, TWOD also has a statewide youth coordinator who concentrates efforts in the area of youth activities, and a minority coordinator who specializes in the needs of the minority communities. The state coordinator for law enforcement, working from the TWOD office in Dallas, monitors law-enforcement activities and coordinates statewide training and awareness seminars for law-enforcement personnel. Additionally, the Texas Lions Clubs have placed a volunteer statewide Lions Club coordinator at the disposal of TWOD.

TWOD, the first organized statewide drug-abuse prevention network, has become a national model, providing guidelines

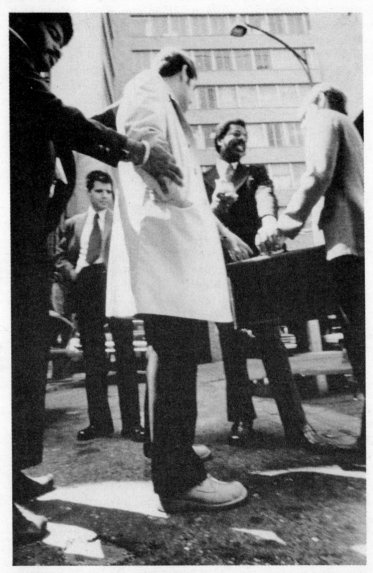

A DEA practice bust comes down.

and assistance to other states and to other countries. The effort in Texas began with a core of dedicated and trained volunteers resulting in a strong grassroots movement. By the end of 1986, TWOD personnel and volunteers had made more than 7,000 community presentations, conducted more than 1,500 workshops for teachers and civic groups, and organized approximately 435 steering committees and coalitions to fight drug abuse in Texas communities.

Through its annual leadership conference, youth-training opportunities, skills for organization, and materials and resources, TWOD has worked with thousands of volunteers organizing local community intervention and mobilization efforts. The thrust is primary prevention—preventing the problem before it starts—and many efforts concentrate on the lower elementary grades.

The main focus of TWOD's education effort continues to concentrate on marijuana because a gross misunderstanding of this drug and its effects on the maturing adolescent remains prevalent in the mind of the general public. Even industry has contacted TWOD on many occasions and asked for more information on marijuana and how it affects workers. In addition, the subject of alcohol cannot be ignored in the discussion of drugs because, of the many psychoactive drugs, it remains the number-one killer. So TWOD has a philosophy of NO "responsible use" messages that promote or support the use of alcohol by minors, or illicit drug use by anyone.

The purpose of the Texans' War on Drugs is to raise public awareness of the effect of youthful drug involvement and help in the formation of groups of citizens who are concerned and willing to work together to reduce drug use by young people. To help create a drug/alcohol-free environment for the children of Texas, TWOD networks among the home, school, and community.

Texas Youth in Action (TYIA) is the youth arm of TWOD. TYIA consists of individual groups of students throughout the state who are active in their schools and communities fighting drug abuse. TYIA's goal is to educate and involve young people in this important endeavor, creating an ongoing effort in which students train their replacements as they move on to

T-shirts, pins, and membership cards are appreciated by kids enlisting in the war on drugs.

college or the work force. This is accomplished through seminars and workshops on local and state levels, educating students about drugs, and encouraging the development of leadership and decision-making skills. TYIA serves as a communication network, with a newsletter mailed bimonthly to more than 1,000 students across the state. *TYIA News* highlights recent prevention efforts by individual groups throughout the state. It also recognizes great ideas, projects to try, and research updates on drug abuse.

For more information, contact:

> Texans' War on Drugs
> 7800 Shoal Creek Blvd. Suite 381-W
> Austin, TX 78757
> (512) 459-1231

Straight, Inc.

Straight, Inc. was founded in 1976 by a group of business leaders and parents in St. Petersburg, Florida. It is a family oriented program that was incorporated as a private, not-for-profit corporation and has been providing substance-abuse treatment services since that date. Straight receives no government funding and is supported by client fees (sixty-five percent) and private donations (thirty-five percent). It is staffed by adult professionals who have been through the program and have subsequently been trained as counselors.

Straight provides intensive treatment services to chemically dependent adolescents between the ages of twelve and twenty-one and their families. The main objective of the therapeutic process is the reconstruction and revitalization of the family system. This approach is used to work with the entire family in order to mend family communication with peer support for each family member. Parents participate through joint and individual counseling and in less-formal rap sessions. A peer group support system provides siblings with an outlet for dealing with the problems associated with having a chemically dependent family member.

While not an in-patient facility, Straight conducts an intense daily schedule of therapeutic sessions. Over the months, clients progress through *five distinct phases* in the treatment cycle.

The *First Phase* starts with admission and lasts for a minimum of fourteen days. The youth does not live at home but with a "host" family that has a child in an advanced stage of the program. This phase explores one's past and how the youth sees his or her world.

In the *Second Phase,* the youth returns to his or her own family at the end of the day. In addition to working on "self," the youth now works on family relationships.

The *Third Phase* adds on another area for self-improvement —namely, school and/or job. In this phase, the youth again faces "do drugs" peer pressure.

In the *Fourth Phase,* the youth continues to work or attend school and begins to have days off to work on constructive use of leisure time and forming positive friendships.

The *Fifth Phase* requires only three days-a-week participation in the treatment process. In this phase, the youth also assists the staff in conducting large group sessions.

A graduate of Straight enters a six-month Aftercare program. The therapeutic tools used throughout the program include a modified version of the Alcoholics Anonymous Steps and Signs that Straight calls the "Tools of Personal Change," plus cognitive therapy techniques that deal with how a person thinks. With at least 800 young people in treatment at any given time, the dynamic of peer pressure in a positive fashion is used to create a new life-style for the clients. Based on annual follow-up surveys, Straight is currently registering a sixty-two percent success rate.

Currently, treatment centers are located in Atlanta, Georgia; Cincinnati, Ohio; Dallas, Texas; Tampa Bay and Orlando, Florida; Stoughton, Massachusetts; Plymouth, Michigan; and Springfield, Virginia. For further information contact:

Straight, Inc.
National Training and Development Center
3001 Gandy Boulevard

St. Petersburg, FL 33701
(813) 576-8929

Quest International

Quest was founded in 1975 completely with private sector funding for the purpose of helping young people face the world's challenges positively. The organization began by bringing together a diverse group of resource people to design a program, "Skills for Living," for high school students. In 1982 it was named by the National Institute on Drug Abuse as one of the three top substance abuse prevention programs in the country. Since then the program has flourished and spun off other projects. "Skills for Adolescents" is one such program. It is aimed at students in grades 6 to 8 and places special emphasis on preventing drug and alcohol use. Since beginning three years ago, it has been used in more than 5,000 North American classrooms and others abroad. The heart of "Skills for Adolescents" is a course that compliments classes in language arts, social studies, health, and related areas, or can be offered as a separate element. The course is comprised of seven units:

1. Entering the Teen Years: The Challenge Ahead
2. Building Self-confidence Through Better Communication
3. Learning About Emotions: Developing Competence in Self-assessment and Self-discipline
4. Friends: Improving Peer Relationships
5. Strengthening Family Relationships
6. Developing Critical Thinking Skills for Decision Making
7. Setting Goals for Healthy Living

A course manual and two books for both adolescents and parents stimulate group discussions and homework. The program also creates a school-community team for support and assistance. Training is provided for school staff who will offer the program on-site. In short, "Skills for Adolescents" is a comprehensive approach to improving the health and well-being of youth through both a multifaceted school program and extensive parent involvement. Students also take part in a service learning component, becoming involved in activities that meet real needs in their schools and communities. Students learn by doing, through service and action working in such efforts as:

- "Buddy" projects in which older students assist and provide guidance to younger students
- Assisting elderly people in the community
- Projects to improve school climate

"Skills for Adolescents" incorporates a clear set of values that includes commitment to a drug free lifestyle, self-discipline, honesty, involvement, responsibility, and compassion. Lions Clubs International and the American Association of School Administrators have been partners in the program. For more information, contact:

Lions-Quest
6655 Sharon Roads Blvd.
Columbus, Ohio 43229
1-800-446-2700 in the Continental U.S.
except Ohio (1-800-233-7900)

DARE

In 1983 the Los Angeles Police Department and the Los Angeles United School District joined together to create DARE (Drug Abuse Resistance Education), now operating in 405 schools. While the program was designed primarily for grades 5 and 6, this year it will be offered to students from kindergarten through grade 8 in Los Angeles. The program costs $750,000 annually, and much of that amount is donated by the Rotary Club, Coca-Cola, and other private donors.

Because prevention requires a change in students' attitude, the traditional approach—teaching students to recognize various drugs and emphasizing the dangers associated with their use—was revised. Fifty-two uniformed officers, carefully trained, teach students to say no to drugs, to resist pro-drug media messages, to build their self-esteem, to recognize and manage stress, and to develop other skills that will help them remain drug-free. In addition, these officers spend time at recess on the playgrounds so that students can get to know them. Meetings are held with teachers, principals, and parents so that the entire school community is informed about and involved in the program.

A formal evaluation conducted by the independent Evaluation and Training Institute has shown that DARE has improved students' attitudes about themselves, increased their sense of responsibility for themselves and to police, and strengthened resistance to drugs. For example, before the program began, fifty-one percent of fifth-graders equated drug use with having more friends. After training, only eight percent reported this attitude.

Questionnaires filled out by students showed that over time they became increasingly negative in their attitude toward drugs, believing that drug use would harm their schoolwork and jeopardize future job opportunities, their relationships with their parents and siblings, and their health. They also were able to make increasingly strong arguments against people who would urge them to try a particular drug. Unfortunately, no effort was made to measure how many students used drugs at the beginning of the training and subsequently quit.

DARE has also changed parents' attitudes through an evening teaching program about drugs, the symptoms of drug use, and ways to increase family communication. Before DARE, thirty-two percent of parents thought that it was okay for children to drink alcohol at parties so long as adults were there. After DARE, no parent reported such a view. Before DARE, sixty-one percent thought that there was nothing parents could do about their children's use of drugs; only five percent reported this attitude after the program.

Due to the high level of acceptance by school principals, teachers, parents, and students, DARE spread from 50 elementary schools to all 347 elementary and 58 junior high schools in Los Angeles. DARE has also been implemented in Mercer Island, Washington, and throughout the state of Virginia where it will reach 15,000 students this year. For more information contact:

> Bureau of Special Investigation/DARE
> Los Angeles Police Department
> 150 North Los Angeles Street
> Los Angeles, CA 90012
> (213) 485-4856

8. QUESTIONS AND ANSWERS

I am often asked to speak to a variety of audiences —sometimes to business and professional groups, once in a while to government officials, but most often to kids and young adults. I think they ask the best questions, perhaps because they really want to learn the answers. (Adults do not always ask questions for this reason.) Here's a handful of the questions I'm most often asked to field. I hope at least a few of them are the ones you might have asked.

Q. Have you ever used drugs?
A. Other than an occasional alcoholic beverage or medical prescription, I have never used drugs. I have too much respect for my mind and body to pollute them. My life has certainly been touched by those who did use drugs, however. About a dozen of my friends have served drug-related jail terms, several have had their careers or health destroyed, and my college roommate was shot and killed while robbing a McDonald's of $145 to support his heroin habit.

Q. How do you handle friends who use drugs?
A. I've been lucky. When I was growing up, drugs weren't as prevalent as they are today, and people knew even then how I felt about drugs. If they used them, it wasn't around me. By the time I got to college, the situation was a little different. People experimented with drugs, even

93

on the teams I was a part of. While I stayed clean, I was aware that others didn't. When I look back at that time, it seems like an age of ignorance. People just didn't know as much as we do now, and, of course, the drugs were weaker. After I began playing professional ball, there have been a handful of times when people have pulled out drugs on the road and I've been in the room. I'm gone. I'm out of there faster than Rickey Henderson stealing a base. I'm frightened. There could be a bust or word could get out and your name is ruined. You're identified by who you hang out with. Guilt by association. Once you're involved with drugs, that's a stigma that lasts a lifetime. Now if I had a teammate or a friend outside of baseball who I knew had a drug problem, I wouldn't turn and walk in the other direction. There's so much at stake: a career, a family, a life. I'd try to help, but ultimately the decision to accept that help would be theirs.

Q. How do you feel about legal drugs, such as alcohol and tobacco?

A. To begin with, no one in my immediate family has smoked. To this day my mother doesn't allow anyone to smoke in her house. She thinks it's worse than tracking dirt onto her white living room rug. So, my first role models got me started in the right direction. I liked sports so much that I never allowed drinking or smoking to be part of my life. My health and physical well-being were too important to me. Despite the cultural acceptance and wide use of alcohol and nicotine, they are bad news.

Approximately one-third of all the deaths in America can be traced to the consumption of these two drugs. The National Center for Health Statistics estimates we spend $120 billion in medical bills for alcohol abuse, almost twice what we spend on the health costs of illegal drug addiction. Smoking-related diseases cost an estimated $43 billion in lost productivity, about fifty percent more than that associated with illegal drugs. We must not let our emphasis on illegal drugs cause us to lose sight of the social costs of legal ones.

Even coffee, not thought to be a drug, has caffeine, a powerful mind-altering component. Caffeine is the most widely consumed drug in the world. More money is spent on the consumption of this drug than on any other. In fact, the only other substance whose dollar value in the world marketplace exceeds coffee is oil. Three out of five Americans drink coffee, and those who drink five or more cups a day triple their chances of heart disease. Recent research also attributes cancer and chromosome changes to heavy use of this drug.

Nicotine and *alcohol* are the two most prevalent gateway drugs for our youth. I don't wish to repeat the myth that users of one drug, such as marijuana, invariably turn to stronger drugs, such as heroin, but experimentation with one drug frequently *does* lead to use of other drugs. The underlying assumption of the drug-progression theory, or substance-use hierarchy, as some investigators have labeled it, is that there are separate steps in drug use. Use of drugs at one step increases the probability of use of drugs at subsequent steps. Typically, youth begin with beer or wine, move on to cigarettes or hard liquor, then to marijuana and other illegal drugs, such as psychedelics and cocaine. A sizable proportion of those who use tobacco, for instance, go on to try marijuana, and the statistics are revealing. A 1980 survey of male high school students showed that only thirteen percent who had tried marijuana had never used tobacco. Twenty-eight percent of the occasional tobacco smokers used marijuana, and sixty-five percent of the regular tobacco users also smoked marijuana.

I am also disturbed by the abundance and power of advertising promoting alcohol and tobacco. Media promotion and peer pressure are the two most decisive factors in persuading young people to try drugs. A recent analysis of tobacco-marketing trends by the Centers for Disease Control indicated that cigarette companies were increasingly targeting their messages to teen-agers. These companies spent $2.1 billion in 1984, a sevenfold increase since 1974, and more than what is spent to

A cocaine processing lab in Colombia.

promote any other product.

One real irony for me when I watch television is to see anti-drug public-service announcements (often unimaginative and uninspiring) alternating with clever and apparently effective commercials for beer. Talk about mixed messages! Bubba Smith, the great defensive lineman, recently had an experience that turned him around. Bubba is famous not only for his prowess on the football field, but also for the commercials he made for a leading beer producer. Last year he returned to his alma mater, Michigan State, for homecoming and witnessed a display in his honor that disgusted him. Many drunken college students were there to greet him. Those on one side of the street chanted "Tastes great!"; those on the other side yelled "Less filling!" Bubba decided this was not the influence he wished to have on America's youth and vowed never to make another such commercial. I wish him continued success with his acting career.

Q. Is there any relationship between drugs of abuse and mental illness?

A. It can be a two-way street. Psychiatric disorders can underlie drug use and drug abuse can lead to a variety of mental illnesses. The incidence of psychological problems is the same, however, for addicts and non-addicts. Abuse of the stimulants—amphetamines and cocaine—can result in schizophrenia, auditory and visual hallucinations, and paranoia. The sedative-hypnotics produce considerable impairment in thinking, anxiety, depression, and a significantly higher suicide rate. Even marijuana is capable of inducing acute paranoid psychoses, usually mild and short in duration, but not always.

It shouldn't come as any surprise that drugs have these effects on the mind. Now that we know more about the delicate chemical balance of the brain, it should be clear that the use of mind-altering substances constitutes an assault upon the body's systems and can throw them out of whack. A single dose of the hallucinogens or PCP can induce "temporary insanity," complete with hallucinations and delusions. There is no doubt that drugs can "blow your mind," or send you over the edge for a time.

Q. How widespread is drug use in America, and how does it compare to the rest of the world?

A. Drug abuse today is prevalent in every segment of our society. No age group, economic class, geographic locale, color, or occupation is exempt. Ironically, the occupation with the highest rate of addiction appears to be medical professionals, particularly anesthesiologists. The easy access of doctors and nurses to potent drugs and extraordinary job pressure help to overcome their training in medicine and addict alarming numbers. They are, however, but a small part of the larger picture. No nation on earth uses drugs, licit and illicit, to the extent Americans do. Indeed, in some countries drug abuse is referred to as "the American problem." Even compared to other Western countries, the U.S. has a high level of personal liberties, privacy, purchasing power, unhindered movement, open borders, and free enterprise. All these factors contribute to high drug use in the U.S.

Q. What do you think are the roots of our society's drug problem?

A. As a culture we are relatively young and impatient. Our attention span is short, so long-term problems appear insoluble. We seem to need a "quick fix" more than other nationalities and are not good at deferring pleasure. We have even enshrined "the pursuit of happiness" as one of the inalienable rights in our Declaration of Independence. "Get rich quick" is certainly not an exclusively American dream, but it seems to be realized more fully here than elsewhere, and drugs can provide quick money. Our media permeate society with the message that drugs can fill most, if not all, our needs. "Better things through chemistry" is more than an advertising slogan; it's a way of life for many Americans. Our pursuit of success often carries a high price tag paid in part through self-prescribed drugs.

On the other hand, we are an ingenious people who have met extraordinary challenges. We like to create options and alternatives and are great believers in our potential. Human problems have human solutions, and if we achieve our capability I see no problem too large for us to handle.

Q.   What about the use of drugs by athletes?

A.   Despite the impression given by frequent accounts in the media, I believe fewer and fewer athletes use illegal drugs. This is not to say that sports does not have a drug problem. It does, but it's getting better. When I think back to a few years ago, just in baseball—proven drug use on teams like the Royals, the Pirates, and the Mets, and strong rumors about the Orioles and the Brewers—it's clear there was a lot more happening on the drug scene then than now.

From what I'm told, amphetamines are still used in football, and so are steroids. Originally, steroids were used in heavyweight sports. Some estimates put the number of weight lifters using them at ninety percent. Now they've even spread to swimming and cycling, and from the professional and collegiate level down to high schools. Their side effects range from cosmetic ones, such as acne or balding, to deadly problems affecting the liver and cardiovascular system. While steroids definitely increase bulk and weight, their ability to strengthen is less certain. One thing is for sure—they do affect temperament. "Roid rage" is no myth. German troops used steroids during World War II to increase aggressiveness.

I've never known anyone in baseball to take steroids; baseball player's drug of choice is alcohol. Beer is as much a part of baseball as the national anthem. After a game it's available in the clubhouse or on the team bus. On the plane, of course, hard stuff is available. At home or on the road, everybody wants to buy you a drink. When I read or hear about old-time baseball players, I gather use was even more extensive then. By talking to some trainers who've been around for a while, I've

Bolivian coca grower and smoker.

learned that baseball players have also gotten their kicks from speed, followed by barbiturates to come down from their high, and even from cough syrup.

Q. Can the "war on drugs" be won?

A. I wouldn't have written this book or be devoting so much energy to fighting drugs if I didn't think so. To win, however, we must be committed as well as compassionate. Like the recovering addict, we all must recognize that our struggle is lifelong. Recovery is a process, not an end. Our previous wars on poverty and for energy independence were lost because we lacked commitment. And, unlike with most wars, compassion is an essential component of the war on drugs. We must provide more help and support for addicts if we are to turn the drug problem around. But do not doubt that we are in a life-and-death struggle for our children and the future of our society. Consider these facts. Only one age group in the U.S. has shown an increase in its death rate since 1900: fifteen-to-twenty-four-year-olds. Fifty percent of these deaths are due to accidents. The second leading cause of death is suicide, up forty percent in the last decade. Homicide is the third leading cause of death in this age group. Drug abuse is a major factor in all three categories.

Q. Is a "drug-free" America a realistic goal?

A. I don't think so. Like batting 1,000 in baseball, it's a laudable goal and theoretically possible, but America has never been drug-free, and I don't see how this will change. If prison authorities in maximum-security institutions cannot keep drugs from inmates, how can we in the outside world succeed where they have failed? We should, of course, work to ensure that certain environments are as drug-free as possible. Students and faculty, labor and management have an obligation to cooperate in keeping drugs out of the school and workplace.

It's important that the goals we set for ourselves be achievable. Politicians who would never speak about a murder-free or rape-free society declaim eloquently about eliminating drugs from our country. We should aim high. Our reach may exceed our grasp, but we should not perpetrate false expectations or be swept up by empty rhetoric.

Q.   What do you think about drug testing?
A.   This is a complex question with no simple answer. In some ways, I understand the push for testing. People are looking for solutions and this appears to be one. Testing has become a buzz word and the cry goes up from government officials, employers, and the general public for more tests. The problems I see with testing are not easily resolved. To begin with, there is the question of reliability. Many labs have a high rate of accuracy, but non-drug substances can show up as drugs even in reputable laboratories. With the huge upsurge in drug testing, many labs with lesser degrees of accuracy have sprung up. They identify non-users as users and they fail to identify users. The most accurate tests are very expensive and seldom used in drug screenings.

Secondly, unless the test is done soon after the drug is used, several drugs are eliminated from the system. Alcohol metabolizes in a matter of hours, opiates within two days, cocaine within three, and marijuana is retained for a week. In chronic pot smokers, even after the drug is no longer being used, the body retains traces of it for up to three months.

Thirdly, there's the question of privacy, of violating the constitutional guarantee against unreasonable search and seizure. While thoughtful people may disagree on this point, the courts have most frequently ruled against mandatory and random testing.

Despite these limitations, I believe testing is appropriate in certain circumstances:

- As a pre-employment screening device
- As a negotiated term of employment
- When there is a legitimate suspicion of drug use

- When public safety or national security is involved

For many people, testing is already a fact of life—NCAA student athletes at numerous schools, employees at a third of the Fortune 500 companies and many other corporations, and armed service personnel. First-time users in the service can be dismissed, although in most cases they are referred to treatment programs. For students at some schools, there are graduated sanctions. A first-time offender is banned for a week or eliminated from a specific event. A second-time offender may be banned from competition for the team, and a third-time offender is out of the program. There is no standard policy in the corporate sector.

I believe employers should be able to demand and provide a safe, efficient, drug-free workplace. If drug testing is required, it should apply to everyone in the company. At the very least, first-time offenders should receive counseling or treatment, not a pink slip. Most progressive large companies have established Employee Assistance Programs to deal with drug problems. A recent Tulane University study indicated such programs had a sixty-five percent success rate.

Q. What do you feel is the most destructive myth about drugs today?

A. I think the concept and phrase "recreational drug" qualifies. I first heard the term in the early 1980s and took it to mean a drug you could use once a week or so over a long period of time and never get hooked. People think you can use these drugs sparingly, judiciously, and they're not going to harm you, particularly if you have a strong constitution. And then when people heard about Len Bias, the Maryland basketball All American, it shocked them. I remember how we Yankees watched and marveled at him during spring training last year. He was in the NCAA Tournament and was the best in the Southeast

Conference, one of the best players in the country. It was clear he took care of his body. A quick and a spectacular jumper, he was drafted by the world-champion Celtics, his dream of playing in the pros only a step away. Two days later he was dead, reportedly of a heart attack. This was incomprehensible. Len Bias, with his physique? The next day, because of my inside track, I heard from the DEA that crack was to blame. Then, the next week, it was Don Rogers of the Cleveland Browns. Cocaine again. People were shocked. With the deaths of two top athletes that week, the myth of recreational drugs also should have died. Unfortunately, the thing that myths seem to do best is persist.

Q. How do you feel about other countries dumping their drugs in America?

A. The most important thing to remember is that if America wasn't demanding drugs, other countries wouldn't be supplying them. It takes me back to biology class—we have a symbiotic relationship with supplier countries, only it's perverted. We're parasites on each other, working to destroy each other. To tell you the truth, I think the supplier countries might have the worst part of the deal. The drug trade causes more violence and corruption there than here. Take Colombia, for instance. If judges or the police can't be bribed, they're killed. Government officials, newspaper editors, even ordinary citizens who protest the drug traffic are gunned down. A few years ago there was a secret meeting in Panama between members of the Medelin Cartel, which supplies about seventy percent of the cocaine that reaches the United States, and the Colombian Ministry of Justice. The drug lords offered to pay off Colombia's $15 *billion* foreign debt if they could cut a deal not to be extradited to the U.S. Colombia said no and recently one of the members of the cartel, Carlos Lehder, was extradited and will soon stand trial.

9. FINAL THOUGHTS

Another Casualty

As I write this final section, finish up spring training for 1987, and prepare for Opening Day in Detroit, I am shocked by yet another casualty in the war with drugs. Dwight Gooden has entered a rehabilitation center for treatment of his cocaine use. Dwight Gooden! It's the dream of America to be on top, so young and so good. The star of the world champions, one of the most idolized athletes in the country—first Rookie of the Year, then a Cy Young winner at age twenty. So much, so soon.

I hope Dwight can turn it around. My heart goes out to him. It's a sad day for me personally. It's a sad day for baseball. The fans treated him as a god, and now I hope they don't blame him for being a mortal. It was his youth, in part, that made him famous, and, ironically, it was his fame that robbed him of his youth. While I don't wish it for him, I can predict that the suspicion of drugs will hang over Dwight for the rest of his life. Let him have a bad game or a bad year and the whispers will be audible.

Considering the Gooden case makes me reconsider the vexing question of drug testing. What is one man's invasion of privacy may be another's salvation. Even though Gooden's fate is uncertain, it has to be better than if he had not been tested. I also wonder if Gooden would have even come to this crossroads if major league players and owners had been able to agree on a policy for dealing with drugs in baseball. How many other players might fall into the void? Right now with no policy and no options, the players are scared that there is no confidentiality, and with hardening public opinion and inflexible management, their careers are over.

Since much will be written about this case in the next few months, I'll stop here with a prayer for Dwight's recovery and return to form. I'd also like to remind you, the reader, that superstar or not, Gooden is just one person in a nation where tens of millions of others would test positive for drugs if they had to undergo such an exam. On the same day that Gooden was front-page news in the main and sports sections of *The Miami Herald,* the top headline in the community section reported ten fire fighters had tested positive for drugs and twenty-four others were suspected. I don't want to sound flippant about this whole affair, but let's remember that baseball is still a game. I'd rather have a twenty-two-year-old fireballer high on drugs than twenty-two firemen who might well be the difference between life and death.

Seeing the Bigger Picture

Nobody but a fool would deny that drugs are a big problem, but I'm not sure if most of us are aware of just how big the problem is, and how it relates to other dismal facts of life in America today. As an example, I saw a recent poll that indicated that white Americans thought that drugs were the nation's number-one problem, followed by the economy. Black Americans felt that jobs were the top problem, followed by drugs. I wonder how many people see the relation between the two problems. Our failure to provide meaningful employment, or in many cases any employment for young people, is a tragedy that contributes to drug abuse. We are disenfranchising, desocializing, and dehumanizing our youth. Lack of self-esteem is the foundation upon which drug abuse develops. To feel good about oneself, one must feel needed. The message to huge numbers of our youth is: "We don't need you."

We must also be more aggressive in seeking the truth. Current factual information is essential to right action. The drug problem is more a symptom than a disease, and any prescription for relief must take this into consideration. We cannot change our children without changing ourselves. Treating a community problem in a society that often lacks a sense of community is difficult. What is needed is not better laws or better programs as much as better people who care more and act on their feelings. Compassion, commitment, and service are the keys to coping with drug abuse. Let's seize the opportunities the drug crisis presents us to work for the creation of a more honest and just society where drugs will not be a major problem.

If we are to turn the drug problem around, families, schools, and communities must broaden their approach, deepen their understanding, and strengthen their commitment. Such an effort must be both aboveboard and across the board. Advertising companies that have profited mightily from selling drugs must now bend their considerable talents to "unselling" them. Drug users must understand that their addiction may begin as a personal choice, but that it ends up affecting many people. Government agencies that previously attempted to stop drug use at the source by eliminating crops in Turkey or Mexico or Thailand must direct more attention to the real source of drug traffic by reducing user demand. I'm encouraged that such actions are now happening. I want my book to speed the process.

The Challenge for the Team

As a ballplayer, I've been on dozens of teams. I've played on ones with lots of talent that couldn't win and ones with little talent that couldn't lose. The key is working together, combining energies to make the whole greater than the sum of the parts. When that happens—it's called synergy—it's exciting. The challenge to individuals, families, schools, and communities is to make it happen. Pool your resources and turn the drug problem around. Take a positive approach to a negative reality. After only a few years of studying drug abuse, I may not yet qualify as an expert on drugs, but I am an expert on being positive.

Every time I step up to the plate, I bring a positive approach with me. Just about the biggest thrill for me on the diamond is tying into a high hard pitch and turning it around over the outfield wall or, better yet, out of the stadium. The ultimate thrill for a ballplayer, I believe, is being selected for the Hall of Fame. I don't know, of course, whether I'll ever be selected, but even if I were, I know the honor would not mean as much to me as playing on the All American team that beats drugs.

We live in a great country with an even greater potential. Let's live up to it. Sometimes before a game when I listen to the national anthem and hear the words "land of the free," I think, not yet, not when so many millions of Americans are slaves to drugs. If all of us dare to dream and rise to our potential, we can alter the course of history and end this drug-abuse epidemic. Let's be the team that meets that challenge.

REFUSAL SKILLS

Three Goals of Refusal Skills

1. Keep Your Friends.
2. Have Fun.
3. Stay Out of Trouble.

Five Steps:

1. Ask Questions, - **"Why … Where"**
   Determine if it is a situation that will involve trouble.

2. Name the Trouble - **"That's …"**
   Tell your friend the real or legal name of the trouble.

3. State the Consequences, - **"If I Get Caught …"**
   Tell your friend what you would be risking. Legal, family, school, self, health, job.

4. Suggest an Alternative; Start to Leave - **"Why Don't We …"**
   Suggest something else to do that is fun, legal, and safe.

5. Keep the Door Open & Leave - **"If You Change Your Mind …"**
   As you leave, invite your friend to join you if he/she decides to come later.

SUPPORT
  Person who supports your saying "NO."

saint paul public schools
INDEPENDENT SCHOOL DISTRICT 625

CRISIS NUMBERS FOR TEENS

ALATEEN 771-2208
CASA (Hispanos en MN) 227-0831
CROSS STREETS (for runaways) ... 647-0410
CHILD ABUSE:
    Welfare Hotline 298-5655
EMERGENCY 911
FACE TO FACE HEALTH
    AND COUNSELING 772-2557
FIRST CALL FOR HELP 291-4666
HIGH SCHOOL CLINICS:
    Central 221-1890
    Como Park 221-1891
    Humboldt 221-1887
    Johnson 221-1886
INDIAN EDUCATION PROJECT 293-5191
INFORMATION AND
    REFERRAL SERVICE 291-4666
MIBCA
    MN Inst. of Black Chem. Abuse ... 291-0299
POISON CONTROL CENTER 221-2113
POLICE 291-1111
SEXUAL OFFENSE SERVICE (S.O.S.)
    (for victims of sexual assault) 298-5898
SUICIDE HOTLINE 347-2222
YOUTH EMERGENCY SERVICE
    (Y.E.S.) 339-7033

10. RECOMMENDED RESOURCES

Publications

The publications in the following list that are followed by an (a) or (b) are available from these organizations:

(a) National Federation of Parents for Drug-Free Youth (NFP), 8730 Georgia Avenue, Suite 200, Silver Spring, MD 20910. Telephone toll-free nationwide 1-800-544-KIDS or, in the Washington, D.C., area, 585-KIDS.

(b) Parents' Resource Institute for Drug Education, Inc. (PRIDE), Woodruff Building, Suite 1002, 100 Edgewood Avenue, Atlanta, GA 30303. Telephone toll-free nationwide 1-800-241-9746.

Adolescent Drug and Alcohol Abuse, Donald I. MacDonald, 1984; Year Book Publishers, 35 East Wacker Drive, Chicago, IL 60601; paperback, $15.95; telephone 1-800-621-9262. A 200-page book on stages of drug involvement, drugs, diagnoses, and treatment. The author, a pediatrician who experienced the problem in his own family, addresses physicians and parents.

Courtwatch Manual. Washington Legal Foundation, 1705 N Street, N.W., Washington, D.C. 20036; enclose $2.00 for postage and handling. A 111-page manual explains the court system, the criminal justice process, Courtwatch activities, and what can be done before and after a criminal is sentenced.

Crack: What You Should Know About the Cocaine Epidemic, Calvin Chatlos, 1986; Perigee Books; New York; paperback, $5.95. The book tells what this dangerous drug is, why it's almost instantly addicting, who is especially vulnerable, how to recognize signs of crack use.

Drug Abuse and Drug Abuse Research, Department of Health and Human Services and NIDA, 1984. The first in a series of the triennial reports to Congress summarizing current research findings in prevention, treatment, all major drugs of abuse, and addictionology. The second report has just been issued this spring.

Drug Abuse in the Modern World: A Perspective for the Eighties, Gabriel G. Nahas and Henry Clay Frick II, editors, 1981; Pergamon Press: hardcover, $37.50. Results and papers from an international symposium held at Columbia University. Covered are the pharmacological and medical aspects of drug abuse, the social aspects, the international dimensions and other issues in almost fifty short papers.

Drug Use Among American High School Students, College Students, and Other Young Adults: National Trends Through 1985, Jerald G. Rachman, Lloyd D. Johnson, and Patrick M. O'Malley, 1986; The National Institute on Drug Abuse, Rockville, MD 20857, ADM 86-1450; single copies are available free. A 237-page book reporting on trends in drug use and attitudes of high school seniors, based on an annual survey conducted since 1975.

Getting Tough on Gateway Drugs, Robert DuPont, Jr., 1984; American Psychiatric Press Inc.; paperback, $7.95. A 330-page book describing the drug problem, the drug-dependence syndrome, the gateway drugs, and ways that families can prevent and treat drug problems **(a) (b)**.

Gone Way Down: Teen-age Drug Use Is a Disease, Miller Newton, 1981; American Studies Press; paperback, $2.95. A 72-page book describing the stages of adolescent drug use.

How to Identify, Prevent, and Guide Treatment of Drug Abuse by Youth, Forest S. Tennant, Jr., Committees of Correspondence, 1985. A handbook focusing on how parents can detect drug use by children and what they can do about it. The effects of commonly abused drugs are described and there is a section on drug-use prevention in athletes.

Kids and Drugs: A Handbook for Parents and Professionals, Joyce Tobias, 1986; PANDA Press, 4111 Watkins Trail, Annandale, VA 22003; paperback, $3.95 (volume discounts); telephone (703) 750-9285. A 96-page handbook about adolescent drug and alcohol use, the effects of drugs and the drug culture, stages of chemical use, parent groups and their creation and maintenance, and resources available to parents and professionals.

Marijuana Alert, Peggy Mann, 1985; McGraw-Hill Paperbacks, $15.95. A 526-page book about marijuana: the crisis, health hazards, and activities of parent groups, industry, and government. **(a) (b).**

Not My Kid, Beth Polson and Miller Newton, 1984; Avon Paperback Books, $2.95; hardcover, $15.95. A 224-page guide for parents to aid in prevention, recognition, and treatment of adolescent chemical use. It is especially strong on overcoming denial and recognizing problems, with numerous personal vignettes **(b).**

Parents, Peers and Pot, Marsha Manatt, 1979; U.S. Department of Health and Human Services; $3.00. A 96-page book that recounts the evolution of the drug culture, the development of the first parent peer group, actions for parents to take, and information on marijuana **(b).**

Parents, Peers and Pot II: Parents in Action, Marsha Manatt, 1983; U.S. Department of Health and Human Services; $1.00. A 160-page book that describes the formation of parent groups in rural, suburban, and urban communities **(b).**

Peer Pressure Reversal, Sharon Scott, 1985; Human Resource Development Center, Amherst, MA; $9.95. A 183-page guidebook for parents, teachers, and concerned citizens to enable them to provide peer-pressure reversal skills to children **(a) (b)**.

Perspectives in Alcohol and Drug Abuse, Joel Solomon and Kum A. Deeley, editors, 1982; John Wright; paperback, $25.00. A series of essays discussing the political aspects of drug abuse, the parallels and incongruities of alcohol and drug laws, a historical review of drug abuse, and a comparison of alcohol- and drug-dependent persons.

Pot Safari, Peggy Mann, 1982; Woodmere Press, New York, NY; $6.95. For parents and teen-agers. Distinguished research scientists are interviewed on the subject of marijuana **(a) (b)**.

Strategies for Controlling Adolescent Drug Use, J. Michael Polich *et al.,* 1984; The Rand Corporation, 1700 Main Street, P.O. Box 2138, Santa Monica, CA 90406-2138; paperback, $15.00. A 196-page book that reviews the scientific literature on the nature of drugs and the effectiveness of drug-law enforcement, treatment, and prevention programs.

Team Up for Drug Prevention with America's Young Athletes; Drug Enforcement Administration, Public Affairs Staff, 1405 I Street, N.W., Washington, D.C. 20537. A free booklet for coaches that includes alcohol and drug information, reasons why athletes use drugs, suggested activities for coaches, a prevention program, a survey for athletes and coaches, and sample letters to parents.

Teen Drug Use, George Beschner and Alfred S. Friedman, 1985; D.C. Heath; hardcover, $21.00. A look at adolescent drug use from the perspective of young drug users and their parents. Why some users have serious problems and others do not. The legal consequences of illicit drug use, secondary prevention. The role of family therapy.

What Works: Schools Without Drugs U.S. Department of Education, 1986; available free by calling 1-800-624-0100 or by mail from Schools Without Drugs, Pueblo, CO 81009. An excellent handbook sketching the extent, development, and effects of drug use, particularly on learning. Other sections include what parents, schools, students, and communities can do, and answers are given on how the law can help and other legal questions.

Free Catalogs of Drug-Abuse Publications

COMP CARE PUBLICATIONS. A source for pamphlets, books, and charts on drug and alcohol abuse, chemical awareness, and self-help. Telephone 1-800-328-3330.

HAZELDEN EDUCATIONAL MATERIALS. A source for pamphlets and books on drug abuse and alcoholism and curriculum materials for drug prevention. Telephone 1-800-328-9000.

Audiovisuals

A Better Place, A Better Time is a 35-minute film, which is a realistic portrayal of the everyday problems caused by adolescent drug use and the struggle of the school and the community to deal with them. The goal of the film is cooperative action—action on the part of everyone involved. It shows how to take those first crucial steps toward building an effective community-wide response to adolescent drug use. Recommended for teacher in-service (A).
Community Intervention Inc., 529 South 7th St., Suite 570, Minneapolis, MN 55415, 1-800-328-0417. Purchase price $495.00 plus $8.50 postage and handling; rental price $95.00 plus $8.50 postage and handling.

Breaking Free is an upbeat 17-minute videotape, set to the music from *Fame,* with an excellent leader's guide. It uses

interviews with young people to show attitudes and facts regarding the drug culture (JHS, HS, A).
PRIDE, 100 Edgewood Ave., N.E. Suite 1216, Volunteer Service Center, Atlanta, GA 30303, 1-800-241-7946. Purchase price $195.000; rental price $30.00.

Dead Is Dead is a 21-minute graphic portrayal of the pattern leading from poly-drug experimentation to addiction. It features explicit withdrawal scenes (JHS, HS, A).
Aims Media, Inc., 6901 Woodley Ave., Van Nuys, CA 91406, 1-800-367-2467. Purchase price $440.00; rental price $40.00.

Drugs, Values and Decisions is a three-part series lasting 30 minutes. Part I, called "When Everybody's Doing It," discusses the widespread dependence on drugs in American culture. It focuses on true-to-life situations to show various problems teen-agers face when "everybody" is taking drugs. Part II, "Dealing with Pressure," examines the motivation of a young woman who uses alcohol to avoid facing her problems. Part III, "One Person's Choice," describes the problems one teen-aged couple faces when the boy begins smoking pot. The filmstrip details the physical and emotional changes the young man goes through when he admits his problem and, with the help of a counselor, kicks the habit (JHS, HS, A).
Sunburst Communications, 39 Washington Ave., Pleasantville, NY 10570, 1-800-431-1934. Purchase price $149.00

Epidemic: America Fights Back (Community Action) is a 32-minute sequel to *Epidemic: Kids, Drugs, and Alcohol.* The film offers solutions to the drug- and alcohol-abuse problem in communities, the workplace, and the armed forces (JHS, HS, A). Purchase price $580.00; rental price $80.00.

Epidemic: Kids, Drugs, and Alcohol is an excellent 27-minute film detailing marijuana, alcohol, and other drug facts. It reveals patterns of peer pressure, attitudes and advertising that contribute to the epidemic of youthful drug use in the

1980s (JHS, HS, A). Purchase price $520.00; rental price $70.00.

NOTE: The two Epidemic films listed above are available from Coronet/MTI Film and Video, 108 Wilmot Rd., Deerfield, IL 60015, 1-800-323-5343.

Feeling Good: Alternatives to Drug Abuse is a 12-minute film narrated by the Rev. Jesse Jackson, who asks that people stop and think about what drugs do to them. He suggests alternative—positive life choices—opportunities to feel good and make constructive things happen (E, JHS, HS).
Aims Media, Inc., 6901 Woodley Ave., Van Nuys, CA 91406, 1-800-367-2467. Purchase price $265.00; rental price $25.00

Get the Message is an 18-minute film that was developed especially for 4-H leaders and teachers as an introduction to discussions on the many "messages" about alcohol and other drugs that young people receive every day. The premise of the film is that well-informed young people are capable of making intelligent decisions (E).
Gerald T. Rogers Productions, 5225 Old Orchard Rd., Suite 23, Skokie, IL 60077, 1-800-227-9100. Purchase price $250.00.

How Do You Tell? is a 12-minute film, using a magical combination of live footage and animation to deal with peer pressure and how to say "NO!" to smoking, drugs, and alcohol. Aimed at the young people who are at the most vulnerable age for initiation into substance-abuse patterns, the presentation encourages kids to adopt the slogan "If it isn't healthy, then don't do it" (E).
Coronet/MTI Film and Video, 108 Wilmot Rd., Deerfield, IL 60015, 1-800-323-5343. Purchase price $310.00; rental price $50.00

Open Secrets, a 20-minute film, is a dramatization that begins in a hospital lounge where three family members wait anxiously for news about a fourth who was involved in an alcohol-related highway accident. The film is designed to encourage adult and adolescent viewers to examine their own attitudes toward drug use, to communicate openly and honestly about this issue, and to take appropriate action in time to prevent harm (JHS, H, A).

Coronet/MTI Film and Video, 108 Wilmot Rd., Deerfield, IL 60015, 1-800-323-5343. Purchase price $495.00.

Sons & Daughters/Drugs & Booze is a 35-minute film describing the drug scene. It emphasizes advertising's subliminal messages telling us that pills, tobacco, and alcohol can solve our problems and make us more desirable. The film suggests ways in which parents can prevent their children's drug-using behaviors without jeopardizing the relationship (A).

Gerald T. Rogers Productions, 5225 Old Orchard Rd., Suite 23, Skokie, IL 60077, 1-800-227-9100. Purchase price $525.00; rental price $75.00

Wasted: A True Story; a 21-minute film, tells about a fifteen-year-old who describes his own story of drug addiction and tells how it nearly destroyed his life and the lives of those who love him. The film has a powerful message, "from one kid to another," describing what the young man lost as a drug addict—self-respect, family, trust, and friends who cared (JHS, HS).

Coronet/MTI Film and Video, 108 Wilmot Rd., Deerfield, IL 60015, 1-800-323-5343. Purchase price $415.00; rental price $50.00.

Key—E: Elementary; JHS: Junior High School; HS: High School; A: Adult

School and Community Resources

ALCOHOL AND DRUG ABUSE EDUCATION PROGRAM, U.S. Department of Education. The "school team" approach offered in this program is designed to develop the capability of local schools to prevent and reduce drug and alcohol abuse and associated disruptive behaviors. Five regional centers now provide training and technical assistance to local school districts that apply. For information, write to the U.S. Department of Education, Alcohol and Drug Abuse Education Program, 400 Maryland Ave., S.W., Washington, D.C. 20202

AMERICAN COUNCIL ON DRUG EDUCATION (ACDE). ACDE organizes conferences; develops media campaigns; reviews scientific findings; publishes books, a quarterly newsletter, and education kits for physicians, schools, and libraries; and produces films. 5820 Hubbard Dr., Rockville, MD 20852. Telephone (301)984-5700.

COMMITTEES OF CORRESPONDENCE, INC. This organization provides a newsletter and emergency news flashes that give extensive information on issues, ideas, and contacts. Provides a resource list and sells many pamphlets. Membership is $15.00. 57 Conant St., Room 113, Danvers, MA 09123. Telephone (617)774-2641.

FAMILIES IN ACTION. This organization maintains a drug information center with more than 100,000 documents. Publishes *Drug Abuse Update,* a 16-page newsletter containing abstracts of articles published in medical and academic journals and newspapers throughout the nation. 3845 North Durid Hills Rd., Suite 300, Decatur, GA 30033; $10.00 for 4 issues. Telephone (404)325-5799.

NARCOTICS EDUCATION, INC. This organization publishes pamphlets, books, teaching aids, posters, audiovisual aids, and prevention magazines especially good for classroom use: *Winner* for pre-teens, and *Listen* for teens. 6830 Laurel Street, N.W., Washington, D.C. 20012. Telephone 1-800-548-8700, or in the Washington, D.C., area, call 722-6740.

NATIONAL FEDERATION OF PARENTS FOR DRUG-FREE YOUTH (NFP). This national umbrella organization helps parent groups get started and stay in contact. Publishes a newsletter, legislative updates, resource list for individuals and libraries, brochures, kits, and a Training Manual for Drug-Free Youth Groups. It sells many books and offers discounts for group purchases. Conducts an annual conference. Membership: individual, $15.00; group, $35.00 (group membership offers tax exemption). 8730 Georgia Ave., Suite 200, Silver Spring, MD 20910. Telephone: Washington, D.C. area 585-KIDS; or toll-free Hotline 1-800-544-KIDS.

PARENTS' RESOURCE INSTITUTE FOR DRUG EDUCATION, INC. (PRIDE). This national resource and information center offers consultant services to parent groups, school personnel, and youth groups, and provides a drug-use survey service. It conducts an annual conference; publishes a newsletter, youth-group handbook, and many other publications; and sells and rents books, films, videos, and slide programs. Membership $8.00 Woodruff Building, Suite 1002, 100 Edgewood Ave., Atlanta, GA 30303. Telephone 1-800-241-9746.

TARGET. Conducted by the National Federation of State High School Associations, an organization of interscholastic activities associations, TARGET offers workshops, training seminars, and an information bank on chemical abuse and prevention. A computerized referral service to substance-abuse literature and prevention programs will begin operating in 1987. National Federation of State High School Associations, 11724 Plaza Circle, P.O. Box 20626, Kansas City, MO 64195. Telephone (816)464-5400.

TOUGHLOVE. This national self-help group for parents, children, and communities emphasizes cooperation, personal initiative, avoidance of blame, and action. It publishes a newsletter and a number of brochures and books and holds workshops across the country each year. P.O. Box 1069, Doylestown, PA 19801. Telephone (215)348-7090.

U.S. CLEARINGHOUSES. (A publication list is available on request, along with placement on mailing list for new publications. Single copies are free.)

National Institute on Alcoholism and Alcohol Abuse (NIAAA), P.O. Box 2345, Rockville, MD 20852. Telephone (301)468-2600.

National Institute on Drug Abuse (NIDA), Room 10-A-43, 5600 Fishers Lane, Rockville, MD 20852. Telephone (301)443-6500.

Toll-Free Information

1-800-COCAINE—COCAINE HELPLINE A round-the-clock information and referral service. Reformed cocaine addict counselors answer the phones, offer guidance, and refer drug users and parents to local public and private treatment centers and family learning centers.

1-800-544-KIDS—THE NATIONAL FEDERATION OF PARENTS FOR DRUG-FREE YOUTH (NFP) A national information and referral service that focuses primarily on preventing drug addiction in children and adolescents. By referral to the caller's "state networker" or a member group in the caller's community, NFP also provides assistance to anyone concerned about a child already using alcohol or drugs. Call between 9:00 A.M. and 5:00 P.M. (Eastern time).

1-800-638-2045—NATIONAL INSTITUTE ON DRUG ABUSE (NIDA), U.S. DEPARTMENT OF HEALTH AND HUMAN SERVICES A national information service that provides technical assistance to individuals and groups wishing to start drug-prevention programs. Currently, the program focuses on the establishment of the "Just Say No to Drugs" clubs.

1-800-662-HELP—NIDA HOTLINE NIDA Hotline is a confidential information and referral line that directs callers to cocaine-abuse treatment centers in the local community. Free materials on drug abuse are also distributed in response to inquiries.

1-800-241-9746—PRIDE DRUG INFORMATION LINE A

national resource and information center, Parents' Resource Institute for Drug Education (PRIDE) refers concerned parents to parent groups in their state or local area, gives information on how parents can form a group in their community, provides telephone consulting and referrals to emergency health centers, and maintains a series of drug-information tapes that callers can listen to, free of charge, by calling after 5:00 P.M.

Information in this chapter was drawn, in part, from *What Works; Schools Without Drugs,* US Department of Education, 1986.